HOW TO DISAPPEAR AND START A NEW LIFE

HOW TO GET A COMPLETE NEW IDENTITY LEGALLY
HOW TO DELETE YOURSELF FROM THE INTERNET

By

Raymond Phillips

Copyright © 2016 - CSB Academy Publishing Company

All Rights Reserved.

No part of this publication may be reproduced, stored in a retrieval system or transmitted in any form or by any means, electronic, mechanical, photocopying, recording or otherwise without the proper written consent of the copyright holder, except brief quotations used in a review.

Published by:

CSB Academy Publishing Company.

P.O. Box 966
Semmes, Alabama 36575

Cover & Interior designed
By

Alex Segrest

First Edition

Table of Contents

TABLE OF CONTENTS 3

FOREWORD 13

INTRODUCTION 16

WHERE TO GET HELP 18

WHY DO PEOPLE DISAPPEAR 20

WHAT IS YOUR REASON FOR
DISAPPEARING? 24

   Disabling Vehicles 27

   Weapons and Firearms 28

DISAPPEARING WITH CHILDREN 30

THINK IT THROUGH 33

THREE MOST IMPORTANT PARTS OF
DISAPPEARING 36

1. Gather up All Your Resources 36

2. Know Where to Go 37

3. Adapt to Your New Life 38

SHORT AND LONG TERM DISAPPEARANCE 40

The Importance of Disappearance 40

Preparation is Essential 41

Long Term Disappearance 41

Withdraw Money 42

Disconnect from Social Media 42

Dealing with Pets 43

Dealing with Your Job 43

Be Thorough 44

Short-Term Disappearance 44

Compile All Identification 44

Destroy Photos and Avoid Cameras 45

Cancel Cell Phones 46

Get Rid of Your Car 46

5 WAYS TO DISAPPEAR FOR THE SHORT-TERM 47

Motorcycle Hangouts 47

New Age Dance Studios 48

Gay Bars 48

Homeless Shelters, Soup Kitchens, and
Churches 49

Domestic Violence Assistance 49

21 TOP DISAPPEARING DESTINATIONS IN THE USA AND OTHER COUNTRIES 51

Sequoia and Kings Canyon National Park in California 51

Providence, Rhode Island, United States 52

Yukon, Canada 53

Richmond, North Yorkshire, England 53

Fermanagh Lakelands, Northern Ireland 54

Inchcolm Island, Firth of Forth, Scotland 55

Arras, France 55

Avila, Spain 56

Sylt, Germany 56

Ikaria, Greece 57

Trieste, Italy 58

Torun, Poland 58

Southeastern Anatolia, Turkey 59

Kiso Valley, Japan 59

Arunachal Pradesh, India 60

Byblos, Lebanon 61

Meknes, Morocco 61

Jambiani Beach, Tanzania 62

Northwestern Tasmania, Australia 62

Kosrae, Micronesia 63

Sao Tome and Principe 64

THROWING OUT THE OLD YOU 65

Destroy Photos 65

Get Rid of Plastic 66

Change Your Appearance 66

Get Rid of Your Car 67

Don't Tell Anyone 70

Decide Where to Go 71

Change Your Spending Habits 71

STEPS TO PREPARE YOURSELF 73

What is a Bug Out Bag and Why Do You Need It? 73

What to Look for in a Bug Out Bag 73

Purpose of a Bug Out Bag 74

Make a List of Essential Items 74

Water and Hydration 75

Food 76

Clothing 79

5 Shelter and Bedding Options 81

4 Ways to Start a Fire 81

16 Must-Have First Aid and Medical Supplies
.... 82

7 Personal Hygiene Must-Have Items 83

6 Core Must Have Survival Tools 84

3 Lighting and Illumination Options 85

4 Communication Tools You Will Need 85

Choosing What to Pack 86

Choosing the Right-Sized Bag 86

    Storage Space 87

AVOID LEAVING TRACES 89

Always Wear a Hat or Cap 89

Seat Covers 90

Avoid the Mail 90

Avoid Leaving Bodily Fluids 90

Clean up After Yourself 91

Choose Where to Eat 92

Avoid Cameras 92

COVER YOUR TRACKS 94

Get Rid of Possessions 94

Disconnect 95

Get Rid of Plastic 95

Lying 97

PROTECTING YOUR PHYSICAL PRIVACY .. 99

Pretexting 100

Ghost Addresses 101

Living Off Grid 102

Prepaid Phones 102

CREATING A NEW IDENTITY 105

Changing Your Name 106

    Finding a New Name 106

    Fill Out a Petition 110

    Attend a Name Change Hearing 110

    Change All Legal Documents 111

Changing Social Security Number 111

    Fill Out an Application 111

    Go to Your Local Social Security Office 112

    Contact Law Enforcement 112

Birth Certificates 113

5 Ways of Using Your New Identity 114

PAPER TRIPPING AND FAKE ID'S 117

Difference Between Paper Tripping and Fake ID's 117

Are the Practices Similar? 117

When Does It Become Identity Theft? 118

3 Types of Ghosters 118

How Do Ghosters Get Their Information? ... 119

Does Ghosting Still Happen? 120

HOW TO CHECK INTO HOTELS ANONYMOUSLY **122**

HOW TO MAKE MONEY WHILE ON THE RUN **126**

    Day Labor 127

    Job Placement Services 127

    Food Work 128

    Work from Home 129

    Warehouse and Factory Work 130

    How to Find Food while on the Run 130

ANONYMOUS BANKING **132**

    The Offshore Banking Process 134

        Basic Requirements 134

        Additional Documents 135

        Setting a Currency 137

        Making Deposits 137

        Withdrawals 138

    Cashing Checks Without a Bank Account 139

HOW TO HAVE FINANCIAL PRIVACY AND SECURITY 142

    Using Bitcoin for Financial Privacy 143

    How Bitcoin Works 143

    HOW TO LIVE UNDER THE RADAR 146

    Leave No Trail 146

    Use an Anonymous Phone 147

    Anonymous Credit Cards 147

    Become a Tourist 147

    Mail Drop Boxes 148

    Live Simply 148

    Enhance Online Security 148

HOW TO DISAPPEAR AND LIVE UNDER THE RADAR: A SUMMARY 150

WIPE YOURSELF OFF THE ONLINE GRID 157

    Lose Your Cell Phone 158

    Use Gift Cards for Purchases 159

Don't Be Social 159

Erase Info Associated with Pictures 160

Encrypt Messages 160

Hide Your IP Address 161

Don't Sign In 161

Don't Look for a Tail 162

Disappear and Deceive 162

LAST WORDS 164

FOREWORD

My name is Raymond Phillips. I graduated in 1996 with a bachelor's degree in criminal justice. After graduating, I worked for a private security firm as an analyst, and during my time there, I was assigned to a large corporate client involved in illegal activities. Unfortunately, I was exposed to their actual crime. Afterward, I found myself running for my own safety and had to disappear seven years ago. Just two years ago, the issues were finally resolved as they got exposed by law enforcement, and that business entity no longer exists, so I was able to reappear.

I sacrificed five valuable years of my life running from them. Over those five long years, I used many innovative methods to keep myself away from everyone and stayed alive. Since I got back, I started a new business as a top-notch privacy expert. I now work as a consultant for a few large multinational businesses.

I started authoring this book while I was away to help people who find themselves in similar situations for whatever reason, but after writing a few chapters, I realized it would be impossible for me to publish it, as I would leave too much of a paper trail that could jeopardize my own safety again. So, I put the project on the back burner and forgot about it.

Recently, I was looking through some of the old files, which I kept on a flash drive and found the file containing those chapters. I decided to complete the book, as I knew in my heart that it could help some truly good and honest people stay safe. But when reading through the files, I realized how much has changed in the last few years, so I decided to rewrite the whole thing.

Here is one quick disclaimer. I am not a writer, never was one, and this is my very first try at writing. So, I will go ahead and ask for your forgiveness in advance in case you find any grammatical or other errors in my work. Just know that the content of the book is authentic, useful and powerful, but the language may not be.

Originally, my intention was to author a two-book series in which, in the first book, I would cover how to disappear and stay safe when you need to. In the second book, I would cover how to get a new identity and start a new life, but I decided to combine both into one book. This way, it becomes a complete guide that covers all aspects.

If you want to learn more about how to delete yourself from the online and internet completely, check out my other book

<u>How to Disappear From The Internet Completely While Leaving False Trails</u>
How to Be Anonymous Online

Thank you for buying my book. Be safe, and may God bless you.

INTRODUCTION

There are many reasons why someone would choose to disappear from society. Some of them are bad reasons, and some of them are good reasons. Like I had my own reasons to disappear for 5 long years.

Just as there are many reasons to disappear from society, there are also many ways in which to disappear from society; some of them good and some of them bad. I had to learn these on my own since I didn't have much time or help to determine the best options, and I needed to get out and start a new life quickly. In this book, we are going to discuss how you can successfully disappear and how you can stay hidden, then we will discuss how you can create a full new identity for yourself legally and start a new life as well as how to disappear from the internet in today's electronic society. All the information I'm going to share with you is what I learned and found most helpful when choosing to disappear.

This book will cover what are considered the best strategies for disappearing, along with the best ways to remain hidden in American society or abroad.

However, I need to start with a word of caution and advice. If you are looking to disappear for a bad or illegal reason, then you should stop reading now. This is about those who have legal and legitimate reasons to disappear, and not those who have committed a crime and want to get away with it by disappearing, or those who want to disappear to get out of a commitment, such as child support. If you are one of these individuals, you will eventually get caught no matter how well you try to disappear. However, if you have a good reason to disappear, keep reading to see how you can do it successfully and start a new life.

WHERE TO GET HELP

In today's electronic society, it is getting harder and harder to hide out in America. There used to be a group of "underground" and "freedom-loving" people who lived off the land and away from the general society. These individuals would often provide shelter, help, and comfort to those seeking to escape society. However, with today's increasing paranoia and dangers, offering to help others is a dangerous proposition. Therefore, if you are considering disappearing, you may want to seek help from a professional organization that assists individuals in specific situations to hide from others.

Just keep in mind that if you are going to use the help of a professional organization, they are going to want you to have a valid reason for running away and hiding out from other people. These professional organizations will report you to the authorities if they believe there is a reason to do so. For example, none of the professional organizations suggested here will help you if you are running from law enforcement. (Note: While a foreigner may get assistance from an embassy in the form of provisional security from police authorities, this is beyond the scope of this book.)

A new class of citizens has developed in recent years. They go by a variety of names, but most commonly they are called "New Age". While many are considered social misfits, they interact with regular society during the day and in their off-hours, they do their own thing. There have always been groups of society that are anti-establishment and socially disassociated; these individuals are always helpful to those on the run. However, to get their assistance, you need to find them first. Once you find them, it is important that you be honest with them. Otherwise, they will be highly unlikely to help you.

Let's consider some reasons people disappear.

WHY DO PEOPLE DISAPPEAR

Most people are under the misconception that those who disappear and start a new life are either criminals, avoiding law enforcement, or wives abused by husbands. While these individuals do, in fact, make up the bulk of those who choose to disappear, there are a variety of other reasons why other individuals choose to disappear.

For most people, disappearing and starting a new life is nothing more than a way to change a life that didn't develop the way they wanted and to get the opportunity to start again. It is a way to forget past mistakes and poor friendship choices, or to have the life they have always dreamed of.

Others are fed up with the lack of privacy in today's electronic society. Some choose to disappear because of various issues with society in general, such as ex-cult members, over-protective families and those trying to go straight from a criminal past. Often, those who were members of a criminal gang find it hard to escape from the consequences. No matter how hard you try to change, the gang can still come after you or track you. This is a serious threat, so people often choose to change their identity to eliminate it.

Another group that chooses to disappear is those trying to get away from creditors. Some even go so far as faking their own death to get away from debt issues or to collect insurance money. While most of us have some level of debt, we try to reduce it. There are, however, some with such huge debts that they have to try another means to clear them. It doesn't matter where the debt comes from, including life priorities, sybaritic lifestyle, health issues and others. This is one reason why many choose to start a new life... to get a fresh start.

As stated above, perhaps one of the main reasons why people choose to disappear and change their identity is to escape an abusive relationship. When in an abusive relationship, people will often ostracize their partner. Whether the abuse is mental or physical, an individual in an abusive relationship needs to find a way not to be tracked or traced. The best way to do this is to change identity and start a new life.

Then there are those who have no choice about whether to disappear and change their identity. The Witness Protection Program is a state-provided service that helps protect witnesses in criminal cases to prevent intimidation and physical harm. Through this program, a witness is given a new identity, physical security and a new place to live. This program will sometimes apply to relatives as well. This can be another common reason for an identity change.

All of the above reasons for disappearing and starting a new life are long-term solutions. Those facing the situations above will disappear permanently and resurface with a permanent new identity. However, there are also those who choose to disappear for only a short term. These are individuals who just need to get their heads straight, take a complete break from everyday life, or take a moment to forget their past and their lives. These individuals need to disappear for a little while, but will return and don't require a new identity.

Lastly, there is the need to disappear due to an external force. These are the individuals who need to disappear after a natural disaster or another event that requires them to start a new life elsewhere (like I had to).

Before you choose to disappear and/or change your identity, it is important to carefully consider why you want to do so and what you want to disappear.

WHAT IS YOUR REASON FOR DISAPPEARING?

Before you decide to disappear and start a new life, it is important to consider just why you need to disappear. Not only can it help you understand, but it will also help you to know to what extent you have to stay hidden.

The resources of the individual or organization that you are hiding from will impact how deeply you need to hide yourself. The degree of motivation that an individual or organization will go to in order to find you will influence how deep your new identity needs to be. It is best to always overestimate the resolve of those who are after you and keep your own estimations reasonable. If you don't properly assess your opposition, you will start behaving in predictable, patterned ways that can be detrimental to you. The predictability of your actions is what will eventually get you caught. Consider a few examples of how this impacts you.

If you are running from police authorities, they have both experience and resources, and they will keep searching for you for a long time. The severity of the crime you've committed will determine how hard they search for you. However, for you, the hunt is very personal. The police know this and will use it against you, just as you must use your knowledge of what they will do to try to find you, so you can know how to evade them.

Hopefully, if you are reading this book, you aren't considering disappearing for illegal reasons. However, let's say you are already in the country illegally and looking to start a new life. You are going to be faced with immigration officials who have historically been understaffed, poorly managed and staffed by individuals with limited training. Unlike police officers, most of these officials want to help people and don't have much time or money to track them down once they are in the country, so their efforts focus on keeping individuals out of the country.

I mention these two examples because they help you see the importance of understanding who is looking for you while you're on the run. Your objective is to disappear completely and start a new, normal life somewhere else. This objective applies not just to the two examples above but to all the other reasons as well. And no matter what your reason for disappearing, you are all going to face the same problems when trying to disappear. However, the individuals trying to find others differ in their resources and tactics. Therefore, knowing who you are hiding from will influence how you choose to disappear and remain hidden.

The greatest influence on your behavior and decisions will be the resources of those looking for you. Depending on resources, you may be able to stay in the same state and simply hide out. However, if the people looking for you have greater resources, you may need to leave the state to completely get away from them. If your opposition also has a great amount of resources, then you should consider planning your escape in a way that you are able to drain as many of the resources as possible. For example, if you are running from an abusive situation, you should see if you can clean out the bank accounts before leaving, so they won't have as many resources at their disposal to find you once you decide to leave.

Another option is to disable vehicles if you need to make a quick getaway. However, if you are going to do this, make sure you do it in a safe, non-violent way. You don't want to commit a crime while disappearing; you'll create a number of other problems for yourself. Consider a few options available to you.

DISABLING VEHICLES

There are a few ways to efficiently disable a vehicle without causing harm. The first option is to add long-grain rice to the radiator fluid. Make sure you do this when the engine is cold to avoid burning yourself when opening the radiator cap. Add as little rice as possible, since it will clog the radiator and damage the engine. Then, when the individual starts the engine, the rice will warp the head, destroying it.

Another option is to add dirt and sand to the engine's crankcase. To do this, you will need to access the oil filler tube, which is usually marked by SAE 30 or 10-40. Add as much sand or gravel as possible. Once the engine is started, certain parts that need lubrication and cooling won't get oiled. This will ruin the engine and cause it to stop working.

Perhaps the quickest and easiest option is the traditional method involving the gas tank. However, with many of today's cars having locking gas caps, this may be difficult. If you have access to the gas tank, simply fill it with sugar. When it is burned with the air/fuel mixture in the engine it will caramelize and gum up the entire engine. However, if you add too much sugar, you will only clog the fuel line, which won't completely destroy the car but will take a while to repair.

There is another resource your opposition has that may be more concerning to you than a vehicle. This is any weapons they may have. Especially if you are fleeing an abusive relationship, you want to deal with any weapons available before choosing to disappear.

WEAPONS AND FIREARMS

If you are comfortable with firearms and know your opposition has them and can use them against you, then you should try to acquire them before you disappear. You can choose to put them in a safe deposit box or any other location your opposition can't access. If you aren't comfortable around weapons, just make sure you keep your finger away from the trigger, and you should be fine. Also, be aware of where you are pointing the barrel of the gun in case of an accidental discharge.

Keep in mind... if you have neighbors around you, or should you live in an apartment, that a bullet can travel through walls, floors, and ceilings. If you are comfortable with weapons, you should probably clear them before transporting them.

If you don't want to keep the firearm around, you can choose to place it in a postal box. When you do this, it will get turned in to the police. From there, the police will either keep it for several weeks while tracking down the weapon's owner or, if it hasn't been used in a crime, destroy it. Oftentimes, if you disappear, even if the police locate your spouse, they won't return the weapon because of your disappearance.

As you can see from this chapter, there are a variety of reasons why individuals choose to disappear from society and change their identity. There are both legal and illegal ways of changing your identity. Some legal ways are citizenship, adoption, and marriage, but you can still do it if you are determined.

It is important that you also give careful consideration if choosing to disappear with children.

DISAPPEARING WITH CHILDREN

If you have to disappear with your children, you should be aware that it will be much more difficult. Children need a very specific standard of living that includes stable housing, meals, and schooling if they are of age. If you don't provide these things and you get caught, then you could be in legal trouble, including possible jail time and having your child taken away from you. Make sure you are aware of all the challenges involved before choosing to disappear with your children.

If there is another parent involved, you could face kidnapping charges if you disappear with your children. Even if the child is yours, you have no right to deny visitation to the other parent unless the court has already revoked visitation rights. However, if there ARE any kind of parental rights, you can be charged with kidnapping at the worst or at the least getting denied legal rights to your children. Be aware of these possibilities before you choose to disappear with your child.

Disappearing with children will also require much more work and effort on your part. It's hard to get a child to give up everything they've ever known. It is also very difficult to prevent children from connecting with old friends and family members, especially if they are older children. It is also difficult to get a child not to talk to people or share information about their past. Make sure you take the time to talk with your children and work with them to understand the importance of keeping your past a secret.

For your plan to work, you need to stay with your children at all times. You don't know what your children are doing if you aren't with them, and this could easily lead to something that ruins your disappearing act. You don't want to spend all your time, effort and money planning a disappearing act only to have an innocent act by your child lead to you getting caught. Keep all of this in mind if you plan to disappear with your child.

As you can see by this, it is important to give careful thought to disappearing before you actually get started. Let's see what you need to consider before disappearing.

THINK IT THROUGH

Before you choose to disappear and start a new life, it is important that you give careful thought to the process and what can happen. Here are a few things to consider before choosing to disappear.

Perhaps the most important thing to consider is the possible legal ramifications of disappearing. Depending on the circumstances and your reasons for disappearing, you could be legally accountable in several ways if you're found. While there are many good reasons to disappear, as we've already discussed, there are just as many bad reasons and bad ways to do so. For example, if a large search party was set up to look for you, then you might have to pay back the incurred costs of the search.

If you choose to disappear to avoid personal debts, you could face fraud and imprisonment charges if you are found. It is an illegal act to stage your own death or disappearance.

If you are planning to escape a gang or domestic

violence situation, then there are legal ways that you can disappear and change your identity. There are a number of government agencies and programs that can help you find a safe, confidential way to disappear and start a new life.

In addition to the legal outcomes that may come from choosing to disappear, you also want to carefully think about what is involved in disappearing and starting a new life.

Perhaps the biggest thing that many don't realize before they disappear is the fact that you will have to do it alone. If you disappear with anyone else or stay connected with anyone, then you greatly increase your chances of being found. If you disappear with a child, you could also be charged with kidnapping or child endangerment if you are found. If you are disappearing because you incriminated another person, then you should take legal action before disappearing in order to protect yourself from allegations that could occur in the future.

Before you choose to disappear and start a new life, you should consider all potential consequences. If you have any type of court charges pending against you, owe personal debt or are trying to avoid personal responsibilities, then you can face serious repercussions if you're ever found. So, think before you act.

You need to consider what you're leaving behind and make all important arrangements before you disappear, so people don't try to come looking for you. After all these careful considerations, if disappearing still seems like a good option, then you will need to start preparing to disappear.

In addition to thinking it through and considering your reason for disappearing, you will need to determine whether your disappearance will be short-term or long-term. Let's take a look at the differences between the two.

Three Most Important Parts of Disappearing

If you choose to disappear and start a new life, there are three key areas to focus on for success.

1. Gather up All Your Resources

First, when you are preparing to disappear, make sure you gather all your resources. Before disappearing, you need to make sure you have everything you'll need in order to survive. Move assets to cash and store money in a secure location until you're ready to take off and disappear. Purchase any supplies you will need with cash. Some necessary items will include the following:

- Backpack
- Warm clothes
- Waterproof items such as matches
- Sturdy Shoes
- Tent
- Sleeping Bag
- Maps
- Compass
- Pocket Knife

If you don't want to rough it in the wilderness, make sure you have cash, necessary papers, and a few basic pieces of clothing before you disappear.

Don't take any valuable or sentimental items with you. Expensive items can get stolen, and sentimental items can be used to find you.

2. KNOW WHERE TO GO

Once you have all your resources ready, you can take off for your new life. However, you need to make sure you know where you're going. There really is no limit on where you can go, except for customs.

If you are thinking about starting again in an international location, you should research the visa or government regulations first. Cheaper countries will make it easier to live longer, but you want to make sure everything is legal.

If you choose to stay in your home country, carefully consider your odds of being found. Make sure no one within 100 miles knows you, and of course, don't go to a spot you used to vacation.

Make sure you plan your destination and commit to it before you leave. You don't want to buy false papers and decide where to go on a whim; this is just inviting disaster. Commit to a specific destination, then plan and prepare for it.

Disappearing is a physically, mentally, spiritually and emotionally difficult process. Make sure you have carefully considered all the pros and cons of disappearing before you decide whether or not it is right for you.

3. ADAPT TO YOUR NEW LIFE

Lastly, once you have arrived at your new destination, you should cultivate new habits as part of your new life. If you don't adopt a completely new persona, you'll easily adopt the old patterns that made you want to disappear in the first place. To do this, there are a few things you can do.

- Buy clothes you normally wouldn't wear.
- Cut and dye your hair a natural color that doesn't attract attention.

- Eat different foods than you used to.

In addition, once you have started a new life, you never want to let your guard down since people can always be looking for you. To do this, you can practice the following habits:

- Start wearing hats indoors to avoid being caught on security cameras.
- Clean up after yourself, don't leave any evidence behind that can be traced to you.
- Stay away from regular mail since it can be used to easily track your location.

While there are many other steps involved in successfully disappearing and starting a new life, these are three of the most important areas to focus on in order to make the process easier.

Let's take a deeper look at some of the things you can do to successfully start a new life after disappearing. We'll start by looking at how you can avoid leaving traces of yourself for others to find.

Short and Long Term Disappearance

As we've already discussed, people disappear for a variety of reasons. Nearly any reason for disappearing is complicated, diverse and personal. Maybe the idea of disappearing is just a casual idea right now, and you're seeing what you can learn, or perhaps you have a legitimate reason for wanting to disappear and need to do so soon. No matter what your reason, you are going to need to consider whether your disappearance is going to be short-term or long-term.

The Importance of Disappearance

Disappearing is not something you should take lightly. If you have anyone close to you, your disappearance can scare them. Even if you don't have anyone close to you, your disappearance can cause a lot of attention among local authorities. In some cases, government agencies and professional services can help you to disappear and start a new life.

However, if you have to disappear on your own and you've given it careful thought, then keep reading for the next step in the process.

Preparation is Essential

While thinking it through is a vital part of disappearing, once you've made the leap of deciding you will disappear, the most essential part is to prepare carefully. You can't expect to simply pick up a suitcase and disappear off the face of the Earth. There are several steps you need to take to successfully disappear, and the more detailed your preparation, the better your chances. On the other hand, there are individuals who need to disappear in a rush and don't have much time to prepare. This is why there are two types of disappearance: short-term and long-term. Let's discuss what each one is so you can see which category you fall into.

LONG TERM DISAPPEARANCE

When it comes to a long-term disappearance, you need to slowly work towards your goal and create a detailed plan. The first step in your process is to start distancing yourself from others and cutting any ties to your old life. This means spending less time with family and friends. Continue this process slowly until you eventually don't see family and friends for a period of time. During this time, they shouldn't expect to hear from you. For this purpose, you will have to learn to lie to people. If you can't get past this first step, then you probably don't have what it takes for long-term disappearance. But if you want to continue, then you can move on to the next step.

Withdraw Money

Your days of electronic money end when you choose to disappear. From then on, you are only going to be using cash, so you want to get all of your money out of the banks. To avoid raising suspicion with banks and law enforcement, you want to do this slowly. Over the course of several months, you can start withdrawing various amounts of cash from all accounts that are under your name.

Once you've drained all your accounts, you will have a nice stack of cash tucked away for when you are ready to disappear. When you don't have any money, the disappearing act can be much more difficult. So, if you don't have any money in accounts, you should start setting money aside now. You want to have as much cash on hand as possible before you disappear.

Disconnect from Social Media

Simply deleting your account won't completely erase

all your information. There are databases that contain your past information, and authorities can access this. However, you still want to start detaching yourself from the social network as much as possible. It is best to delete anything attached to an online account. Again, you want to do it slowly; otherwise, people tend to take notice.

Dealing with Pets

If you have pets, it's probably best to take them to a shelter if you don't have a friend or a neighbor who can adopt them under another pretext. You shouldn't attempt to take a pet with you when you try to disappear. Pets tend to raise attention, make you more recognizable and take more time, effort and money to care for. No matter how much you love your pets, you can't take them with you when you disappear.

Dealing with Your Job

Just before you choose to disappear, you need to have some time to make any last-minute preparations. Be sure to give yourself a head start before people question your absence. If you haven't quit, your current employer will be the first to realize you've gone missing. So if you don't want to quit, you should at least request some time off so no one suspects you are missing for a while, and you get a decent head start.

Be Thorough

If you are renting, try to avoid a lease so landlords don't try to look for you. Or, if you have to, try paying a few months in advance to give you a head start when you do leave. You should do this a few times before you leave, so your landlord will be used to you paying several months in advance and not question it. Tell your neighbors you're going on vacation. Make sure you have everything planned out, so no one comes looking for you until you've had time to get far away and start on your new life.

SHORT-TERM DISAPPEARANCE

If you don't have a lot of time to plan your disappearance and need to get away right away, then there are a few steps you can take to give yourself a decent chance. However, if you can afford a long-term disappearance, that is your better option for success.

Compile All Identification

Gather up anything that can be used as identification: school ID, driver's license, birth certificate, social security card and bank statements. Anything with your name and a picture on it should be gathered in one place.

There are different theories and ideas on what you should do with these documents. Some sources tell you to keep them and stash them somewhere safe, while others tell you to get rid of them.

Whatever you decide to do with your IDs and personal documents is up to you, but be thorough. Don't leave anything behind that can be found and used to locate you. The goal is to leave no trace behind.

Destroy Photos and Avoid Cameras

This may seem like a drastic step, but photos can be used against you in the case of a short-term disappearance. When people become concerned about your disappearance, they will start looking for you. It will be a lot more difficult to find you if there are no recent photos of you.

If you eliminate photos and avoid getting spotted by cameras, then you are sending the message to family and authorities that you disappeared on purpose. If authorities thought you were kidnapped or murdered, then they are going to try a lot harder to locate you.

Cancel Cell Phones

You won't need a cell phone when you're on the run. When you start a new life, you won't be on social media as often. Even if you really need a cell phone, you will be getting a burner phone under your new identity. So, before you disappear, make sure to cancel your cell phone service.

Get Rid of Your Car

Perhaps the most traceable and recognizable item you have is your car. You can sell your car for some quick cash, or you can abandon it in a part of town where it will get stolen. Either way, you want to get rid of your car fast before you disappear to start your new life.

5 Ways to Disappear for the Short-Term

Motorcycle Hangouts

For these individuals, your best option is to befriend them. You don't want to lead them on and just use their help; you want to befriend them. Then they will be able to hide you and help you start a new life with a new identity.

When you first find these individuals at their hangouts, you want to buy some drinks, talk, express your viewpoint and get to know individuals. Express an honest interest in their way of life; you may even find something that appeals to you. Eventually, you can let some of them know that you are looking to hide out and start a new life, so that you will be able to get their help. Ask where you can find a place to stay or where you can find some work, and this may lead you to a new way of life with some new friends.

Motorcycle riders have a rough reputation, and you do need to be aware of this. If you're on the run and want a place to hide, you have to play by their rules. They are often good people, worthy of being your friends and willing to help, but you need to fit into their society first. Many motorcycle groups today aren't what you might picture from movies and television; rather, most have regular jobs during the week and hang out on weekends when they can.

New Age Dance Studios

Here you will find the younger crowd, and while they may not have the resources to help you directly, they are likely to know where you can go and who is available to help. Make sure they know right away that you are looking for some help and ask to be pointed in the right direction.

Gay Bars

This is the place to go while on the run, and you only need a quick meal or a place to spend the night. Most individuals in gay bars are looking for companionship, whether the other individual is gay or straight. If you're interesting and have stories to tell, then most will be willing to give you a place to stay for a few days in exchange for sharing your stories with them. The key here is not to be shy and not to overstay your welcome. Offer to leave occasionally and do so when asked.

HOMELESS SHELTERS, SOUP KITCHENS, AND CHURCHES

You will find these locations in pretty much any moderate to large-sized city. They are typically run by the State government or a religious organization. While most won't ask questions, they will typically want to make sure you don't have weapons or drugs before allowing you to stay. You may also be able to get some work in the kitchen or dorms. If you show a willingness to work, they may help you find a paying job, which you will need to do if you are going to start a new life.

DOMESTIC VIOLENCE ASSISTANCE

If you are running away from an abusive relationship, there are many options for help available to you. Perhaps the best option is to go to a shelter in another state. If you have children and you can't take them on the run with you, you can call 1-800-4ACHILD, and they can help you find safe options for your children. There is also the National Domestic Violence Hotline at 1-800-799-7233.

It is important to note that before you run away,

you should document any allegations of abuse. Perhaps the biggest difficulty is that if you are trying to run away from an abusive relationship, is that you will also need to deal with legal issues at the same time. The shelter you go to should be able to assist you in this area.

Once you know what type of disappearing act you are going to do, you want to start considering where you are going to disappear to. Let's take a look at some ideas to get you started.

21 Top Disappearing Destinations in the USA and Other Countries

If you are considering disappearing and starting a new life, you may want to start somewhere new. While most people want to stay close to where they grew up or just have a chance to start again, others want to completely get away from their lives and start somewhere new where no one will recognize them. Then there are those who only want to disappear for a little while to "find" themselves and have a change of pace. No matter what your reasons for disappearing are, if you want to know the best places to stay under the radar, then consider some of the following destinations.

Sequoia and Kings Canyon National Park in California

This is good for those who don't want to leave the country. Most people associate California with sun and beaches, but California is also well known for its trees. Not only does California have the tallest coast redwoods and the oldest bristlecone pines, but it is also home to the largest tree by volume in the Sierra

Nevada. Many of these can be enjoyed at the famous Yosemite National Park, but if you want a quieter change of pace, then you can head south to Sequoia National Park or Kings Canyon National Park.

In addition to the giant redwood trees, these parks feature a cleft deeper than the Grand Canyon, numerous trails, and caves. It also features the highest peak in the United States outside of Alaska. So there are plenty of places where you can go to either get away from it all and disappear for a while, or, if you truly want to rough it in the outdoors, you can easily disappear off the grid and live off the land in the areas around here.

Providence, Rhode Island, United States

This is another option for those hoping to stay in the United States, but on the eastern coast. Rhode Island is the smallest US state, more like an English county. Providence is the state capital and shares many of the same qualities as Boston, which is only an hour's drive away. However, Providence is about a quarter of the size of Boston. The city has a strong student influence thanks on Brown University and the Rhode Island School of Design. Downtown Providence is also the only area in the US to be entirely listed on the National

Register of Historic Places. The neighborhoods here range from the stately 18th-century homes to colorful Italian and Portuguese communities. An excellent place to hide under the radar while still feeling part of a larger community and watching out for those around you.

Yukon, Canada

If you want to get out of the country but not too far, consider Yukon, Canada. This is where Canadians go when they feel too crowded. This wilderness area is near the border with Alaska. It is twice the size of the UK, but has far fewer residents. While this region experienced a population surge during the gold rush days of the 1800s, there are only a few reminders of that era in small towns. It features some of the largest polar fields outside of the polar regions. Whether you want a scenic adventure to get away for a little while or you want to really disappear and rough it in the wilderness, this is the destination for you.

Richmond, North Yorkshire, England

There are many places called Richmond throughout the world, from a London borough to the state capital of Virginia. However, we are talking about the original Richmond just outside of the Yorkshire Dales National

Park along the River Swale. It is home to the Richmond Castle, one of the oldest stone fortresses in the country. However, the true heart of the town is Market Place.

This place has an outdoor market every Saturday with a permanent indoor market. The quaint little town features cobbled streets lined with beautiful little cottages. A nice place to hide out, like Rhode Island, where it is small enough to know the local population and yet large enough to successfully hide yourself.

Fermanagh Lakelands, Northern Ireland

This is the best destination for someone who wants something blissfully unhurried, although it did gain some fame for the G8 summit. This area is about one-fifth water, and most of it is a lake split into two parts. The upper part of the lake is a maze of over 150 islands, while the lower part is a more traditional open lake. Many of the islands in this area have a long legacy. For example, on Devenish Island, there is an Augustinian monastery, and on White Island, there are six enigmatic Celtic stone figures. More modern history is seen in stately homes such as Castle Coole and Florence Court. The waterways are full of trout and salmon. With so many little places, it is easy to find a place off the grid to hide and live off the land.

Inchcolm Island, Firth of Forth, Scotland

While this island is a pretty small sliver of land, the ruined abbey on it feels like your typical remote Scottish island. This island is located about a half-hour boat ride from Edinburgh. The ruined abbey on the island houses the best-preserved monastic complex in all of Scotland. The abbey was founded in 1123 by Augustine monks, and it offers beautiful views. In addition to the abbey, there is a Macbeth Festival held here, and the island is dotted with tunnels, lookouts, and bunkers from use as a garrison in both World War I and World War II. Today, the only permanent inhabitants of this island are animals. Making it the perfect spot for a short-term disappearing getaway.

Arras, France

Most people know of this small town in northeastern France because of its proximity to the front lines of World War I. However, the town boasts beautiful squares with a vertiginous belfry and colorful arcades.

The exuberant town today defies its somber history. There are two ancient market squares, the Grand Places and the Petite Place, surrounded by Flemish-Spanish houses from the 17th and 18th centuries.

Beneath this town, there are historical tunnels that were used as British command posts, hospitals and barracks in World War I and now blossom each spring into a beautiful garden. A wonderful place to disappear off the radar.

Avila, Spain

This town is set on the cool, high plains of Castilla y Leon in central Spain and features a historic bastion. The main feature of this town is the bastion, with thick walls 12 meters high that surround it. It is interrupted only by a series of embellishments, such as eight gates and dozens of towers and turrets. This bastion was built in the 12th century atop the remains of Roman and Muslim battlements. Today, there are some of the best-preserved medieval walls, and you can even walk along part of them. Further around the town are snow-dusted mountains. Inside, there are quiet medieval streets. A nice place to start your new life.

Sylt, Germany

This town is popular with German tourists, and it's easy to see why. It is a large, anchor-shaped island in the North Sea featuring a civilized drinking and dining scene.

However, if the party life isn't your thing, there are still plenty of spots with quiet beauty where you can enjoy flower-thick gardens and lighthouses overlooking green meadows and sand dunes. To the west, you can enjoy miles of secluded fine-sand beaches and wild surf. To the east lies the Wadden Sea, with natural tidal mudflats. In the town itself, there are a number of eateries ranging from bistros to Michelin-starred restaurants, so you have no shortage of fine places to dine. The perfect all-around place to disappear and start a new life.

Ikaria, Greece

If you want someplace to disappear where you can eat, drink and just unwind, then this little place in Greece is the perfect place. This is a place where the average person lives easily to 100.

This likely has to do with the place's serenity and opportunities to unwind, such as the hot springs. This hilly isle lies in the northeastern Aegean Sea and is largely bypassed by tourists. A good chunk of the island is crumbling ruins, secluded bays and small villages where residents gather. Ikaria is a vineyard-rich town with easy-going individuals.

So, for an out-of-the-way place that works well for short disappearances to get away from it all, or for a long-term place to disappear off the radar, this is a great option.

Trieste, Italy

This city can easily be the best place in all of Europe. This little piece of Italy is mostly surrounded by Slovenian territory and was once Austria's main cosmopolitan port.

The town is a mix of Latin, Slavic, and Germanic cultures. You can find this through a mix of food choices. The town also features graceful 18th-century districts straddling a Grand Canal, as well as richly decorated neoclassical churches and synagogues. A nice cultural town to disappear to.

Torun, Poland

While many of Poland's fine towns were destroyed during World War II, the walled medieval port of Torun on the Vistula River escaped mostly intact. Today, it continues to be bypassed by most tourists, so they don't get to appreciate the Gothic architecture throughout the town.

The architecture in this town is some of the best-preserved in northern Europe, from the ornately decorated houses to the red-brick buildings of the old town. Some standouts include the towering cathedrals, the medieval ruins of the castle and walls, and the 14th-century town hall, which offers sweeping views of the city. A nice historical place to disappear from the world and start a new life.

Southeastern Anatolia, Turkey

This region in Turkey is vastly different from the cosmopolitan Istanbul or the laid-back coastal regions. At one time, this frequently passed-up region of Turkey was the northern frontier of Mesopotamia. Today, it is a region filled with sites dating back far in human history. For example, the stone circles of Gabelli Tepe are thought to contain the world's oldest temple. An equally beautiful area is Mardin, where golden stone houses overlook sunbaked plains and colossal ancient statues.

Kiso Valley, Japan

This thickly wooded Kiso Valley was the main route through central Japan about two hundred years ago. Today, it is more out of the way. As a result, it preserves a number of old post stations along the mountain road, Nakase do, that runs from modern Tokyo to Kyoto. The most beautiful of these stations is Tsum ago, which has limited modern development and still features traditional dark-wood, lattice-fronted houses along a car-free main street.

There is plenty to see and do in this small town. If you take the entire five-mile hike along the route, you will pass through farmland, forest, and waterfalls. A nice time capsule to disappear into.

Arunachal Pradesh, India

This is the land known for dawn-lit mountains and is high on the list for Shangri-La candidates. This area sits at the confluence of India, Bhutan, Tibet and Burma. Historically, this area has been inaccessible from any country and is so remote that a few of the Himalayan peaks there haven't been named or climbed. Today, relaxed travel restrictions and improved infrastructure allow this extraordinary place to be explored.

Here you can enjoy nature reserves teeming with diverse wildlife not seen anywhere else in India. The forests are home to delicately tattooed tribal people. The mountain valleys are filled with majestic Buddhist monasteries, including the world's largest, Tawang Gompa. An adventurous place to start your new life.

Byblos, Lebanon

While at first glance this may seem like nothing more than a simple, picturesque fishing harbour, you will also find a lot of history in this town. This serene little town north of Beirut has been around for quite a while. Some even claim it is the oldest continually inhabited town in the world.

This town has been featured in the Bible, conquered by Crusaders and was the source of the modern alphabet. Today, all these layers of history are well represented in the ruins of ancient temples, tombs, and Neolithic houses. Perhaps the three best sites are the reconstructed Roman amphitheatre, the 12th-century Crusader Castle, and the restored medieval souq, which features everything from antiques to fossils.

Meknes, Morocco

Meknes is the fourth-largest and also the most modest of Morocco's imperial cities, making it often overlooked. The city is a mix of narrow streets and grand buildings. It is nestled among the fertile plains of the Middle Atlas Mountains. The city includes numerous palaces, 25 miles of historic walls, dozens of mosques and the vast, ornate tiled Bab el-Mansour gate. Most of these sites date back to the 17th and 18th centuries. It also features the largest Roman ruins in the country.

Jambiani Beach, Tanzania

This is a clear standout in the country. It is located along the island's east coast, and it is protected by offshore reefs. This particular beach is long and palm-fringed with fine coral sand that slopes into a turquoise sea. This beautiful landscape is one of the quietest places on the East Coast and offers a glimpse into rural Zanzibari life. Along with the vibrant fishing village, there are a number of coral-and-thatched houses. During the day, you can observe age-old daily rituals, including the drying of seaweed and fishing from outrigger canoes.

Northwestern Tasmania, Australia

Australia's island state of Tasmania has long been known for its apples and is quickly becoming the best stop for the country's food. The beautiful, unspoiled countryside and pristine waters provide a wide range of local produce. A number of restaurants in the area offer delicacies that are hard to beat.

Among the rolling hills, you will find farms full of cherries, raspberries, and even organic salmon. Nearby King Island is home to bries, cheddars and blue cheeses, along with crayfish and oysters. Throughout the area, there are over fifty varieties of honey. A wonderful area to spend your new life.

Kosrae, Micronesia

You are going to need a lot of time to reach this island since the nearest international connections are Honolulu and Guam. Kosrae is the easternmost island in a chain of 607 that make up the Federated States of Micronesia.

This isolation is one of the island's biggest benefits. It is surrounded by coral reefs, making it one of the most undisturbed areas in the Pacific Ocean and sheltering a variety of marine life.

In the summer, the visibility of the water can be 60 meters, enough to see the submerged remains of an American flying boat and a Japanese freighter that sank in World War II. The interior of the island is a rainforest, and it has delightful beaches. A nearby islet, Lelu, features jungle-covered ruins that resemble a smaller version of the lost city of Nan Madol on the main Micronesian island of Pohnpei.

Sao Tome and Principe

These islands like to live life slowly and calmly. This one-time Portuguese colony was formed from two islands in the Atlantic. São Tomé is a tropical island right along the equator. The volcanically formed interior shelters rainforests and a wide range of plant and bird species. The smaller neighbour is Principe. Both of these islands produce some of the world's best cocoa and coffee. The modest capital features Portuguese-era buildings, beaches and hiking trails through a rugged landscape.

While there are plenty of other destinations where you can disappear to, these are just a few ideas to get you started on the endless possibilities of destinations where you can start your new life.

Once you are ready to disappear, make sure you have everything in place, and to do this, get rid of the old you so you can start building your new identity.

Throwing Out the Old You

Before you choose to disappear, it is important that you get rid of the old you as much as possible. In order to successfully disappear, you need to make it seem as if you never existed in the first place. This means you want to consider doing as many of the following tips as possible to help you disappear.

Destroy Photos

You want to destroy all photographs that you have access to before disappearing. This includes any photographs your family may have. While family members may or may not support your opposition, you still don't want to have photographs of yourself that can be shown around various places to help track you.

Even a family that is supportive of your disappearance can be forced to support the opposition through the threat of law or physical violence. You want to limit your opposition to just working with artist renditions of you, so it is harder to locate you. Old photographs of you are okay as well, but you don't want your opposition to get a hold of any up-to-date photographs of you.

Get Rid of Plastic

You want to get rid of everything you own except cash. You especially want to get rid of all your credit cards. The moment you use credit cards or debit cards while trying to disappear is the time when the authorities or private investigators will be able to find you. Before you disappear, it is a good idea to empty all your bank accounts anyway.

The best rule of thumb is that any card with your name on it and a magnetic strip can be used to track and find you. Don't even take a card with you for emergencies since you may be tempted to use it, and you don't want to give away your location.

Change Your Appearance

You want to get a whole new wardrobe. Purchase clothes that you normally wouldn't consider wearing. Destroy your old clothes so they can't leave a trail back to you.

Get Rid of Your Car

Abandon your car. This doesn't mean you need to drive it into the nearest body of water. Rather, you can abandon your car in such a place that you know it will be stripped and sold by thieves, as long as you are sure you can safely walk out of the dangerous neighbourhood. If you are going to abandon your car, you may want to leave the pink slip in the glove box or leave a door unlocked, so it is easier for thieves. It is better for the car to be taken entirely by a thief than to be picked apart and left on the street for the police to spot. You might as well just leave the keys in the ignition. This way, you can easily and efficiently get rid of your vehicle and avoid having it traced back to you.

Once you've got rid of your vehicle, you will need to be careful how you plan to disappear. When you choose to disappear, you should never use a taxi. Taxies have drivers and dispatch, with records of pickup and drop-off locations as well as descriptions of their passengers. Rather, you may want to consider buying another vehicle. If this is the case, you want to buy something cheap and simple. This way, there aren't many questions, and hopefully you won't have to provide any identification.

When buying a new vehicle to disappear in, there are a few things to check to avoid getting pulled over by the police.

- Make sure the back license plate has a current registration.
- Make sure the exhaust doesn't visibly smoke.
- Make sure turn indicators are working.
- Make sure the headlights are working.
- Make sure the windshield has no cracks.
- Make sure there are no broken or missing brake lights.
- Make sure there is an ignition key.
- Make sure there is a pink slip.

Most importantly, you want to make sure you aren't buying a stolen vehicle. Make sure the VIN number on the pink slip matches the VIN number on the metal plate mounted on the dashboard under the windshield wiper. The pink slip should also match the license plate number. If something doesn't match, then you shouldn't buy the car in case it is stolen.

You also don't want to borrow a family or friend's car. Many highways and streets have cameras that can track the make and model of vehicles. Even if you aren't using your own car, most opposition, such as investigators and police, will not look for known vehicles you might be using.

It is important not to fill up your new car with personal belongings. If you look like you're packed up with possessions, then it can be suspicious for police officers. You should already discard everything you own before disappearing, but even if you take a few things with you, they should be able to fit in the trunk. Even if you aren't stopped by the police, you can also look suspicious to a police officer if there is a report of you missing. When you are trying to disappear, it is important to blend in with your surroundings.

If you do get pulled over by the police, remember that police work off profiles. Police officers are trained to spot unusual individuals and situations. If you look like someone simply going to work or running errands, it won't raise a police officer's suspicions. But if you have a number of items crammed into your car, they are going to look twice and try to match you against any profile they have of missing or suspicious people.

For this reason, you also want to make sure you are as outward composed as possible. Don't act frightened, anxious or worried. Rather, just try to be carefree and outwardly composed so you don't give off the wrong signals to a police officer. Focus your thoughts on being a productive new member of society and not on the life, family and friends you have left behind.

While running from the police is certainly not something you want to do, doing it in a car or on a motorcycle is far worse than running on foot. If you try to run in your car, then you might injure yourself or someone else, and the police will be more motivated to stop you. With a vehicle, it is very difficult to escape the police. You won't stand much more of a chance on foot, but it does give you better odds. However, the best option is to see if you can manage to talk your way out of it.

Don't Tell Anyone

Perhaps the most important part of disappearing is avoiding telling anyone about your plans. Once you do disappear, avoid asking anyone you know for help. You want to be completely cut off from contact with family and friends. Police and private investigators are likely to keep tabs on your family and friends in the hopes that they can be led to you.

Decide Where to Go

When you disappear, it is important that you don't go anywhere too obvious. You shouldn't talk about the place you want to go, and you certainly shouldn't disappear to a place you desire to visit. You should also avoid predictable areas like Las Vegas or Los Angeles. If you are running from an abusive situation, you definitely want to go to a shelter in another state. For some good destination ideas, consider the chapter in this book on the best under-the-radar destinations.

Change Your Spending Habits

Be prepared to alter your spending habits once you disappear. Once you get rid of your old self, you will develop new patterns and habits. Don't go to the same bars or restaurants, so you don't fall into a predictable pattern that people can trace. Don't even go to the same fast food restaurants you used to frequent to avoid getting spotted by people monitoring places you prefer. Rather, make sure you develop all new styles and habits so you can completely change your life and become someone different.

In addition to changing a lot of things, you want to be prepared to go at a moment's notice. The best way to do this is to have a bug-out bag ready to go for when you need to make a run for it.

Steps to Prepare Yourself

What is a Bug Out Bag and Why Do You Need It?

A bug-out bag is something everyone should have on hand. Basically, it is a kit in a bag that is easily accessible. An individual needs a bug-out bag for a variety of reasons. Any individual could use a bug-out bag in the event of a natural disaster to get away quickly.

On the other hand, for individuals trying to disappear and live under the radar, a bug-out bag is something they can take if people are getting too close to finding them and they need to get up and go quickly. If you are going to have a bug-out bag, then you need to consider a few things to get the right bag and pack it with the appropriate supplies.

What to Look for in a Bug Out Bag

A good bug-out bag needs to meet three specific requirements:

Durability

Intelligent Design

Customised to Body Dimensions

It needs to be durable, so it holds up when you need to bug out quickly. It needs to be intelligently designed so you can access all of the gear quickly and easily. Lastly, you want a bag that won't slow you down or wear you out in case you need to travel far and fast.

Purpose of a Bug Out Bag

While this was briefly discussed in the introduction, it is important to understand the purpose of a bug-out bag to make the best choices. A bug-out bag shouldn't be used as a mini house to carry unnecessary stuff. Packing too much in your bug-out bag will simply slow you down and make it more difficult to get away. It is best to consider absolutely what you need to pack before you actually look into buying the pack itself.

Make a List of Essential Items

Before you choose a pack, you want to determine what you will put in it. Below, we'll discuss a checklist of some of the most essential items you should have in your bug-out bag, but it isn't a complete list of all possible items. Even the list below will be too much weight, so you will have to be selective and only pack items you know you will need or are specific to potential survival in your bag.

WATER AND HYDRATION

Perhaps the most important items to focus on are those related to water and hydration. Whether you are escaping for survival after a natural disaster or you are trying to disappear, you don't know how long you will need to stay away from potential shopping sources. Water is the key to survival, so you want to make sure you are able to have plenty on hand. Here are a few water and hydration tools you may want to consider:

Stainless Steel Water Bottle - A good water bottle is important, and the best you can have is a stainless steel one and not a plastic one. The easiest way to purify water is to boil it, so it's safe to drink. A stainless steel water bottle allows you to refill and boil/filter/purify your water as long as needed.

Water Purification Tablets - If boiling is too time-consuming, then you may want to have a few water purification tablets in your bag. These tablets will treat water fast and allow you to purify your water while keeping on the move. In addition, these tablets are lightweight, so you won't have to worry about carrying extra weight on the go.

Portable Water Filter - A good filter can remove all particulates from water, but a great one will also remove bacteria. So, another item to consider is a portable water filter that not only cleans but also purifies your water. Water filters are small and portable, so they will save you weight and space.

Expedition Jerrycan Filtration System - While this is a larger filter that will have to hang on the outside of your bag, it is a good option if you need a bug-out bag for a family. It can provide enough clean water for a family of four for nearly a year.

FOOD

The second most important item to water is food. These are two survival necessities, whether you are bugging out for a long time or just a short time. It is important to pack calorie-dense food. There are a few food items that can help keep you healthy and maintain your stamina while on the run. You also want to focus on light and easy-to-prepare foods.

Although for those looking to disappear for the long-term and live off the grid, you may want to focus on living on what the land can provide and just bring enough food to get you by until you can start producing your own.

Calorie-Dense Food Bars - Any food bar will work, as long as you read the label and choose the ones that provide the most calories per bar. The best food bars for your primary energy needs depend on your physical activity. Typically, a man requires about 2,400 calories. A food bar is also a good idea because it has a decent five-plus years shelf life without adding much weight to your bug-out bag.

Freeze-Dried Meals - This allows you to have a hot meal in a lightweight pouch. You only need a few minutes to prepare them; just add boiling water, stir and eat.

Military Meals (MRE - Meal, Ready to Eat) - These meals are a little heavier and take up more room, but they're good if you want a complete, healthy meal.

When it comes to packing your food, you also want to keep in mind something to eat with. There are a number of small and lightweight survival tools that allow you to eat your food without having to use your hands. You want utensils that combine multiple tools and are durable since you will probably be using them quite often.

You won't need much in the weight of dishes. You might only need a small collapsible bowl for serving and eating. This way, you have something small that doesn't take up much space.

If you choose to disappear and live off the grid, you may want to pack some items to help you start growing your own food. Or you can purchase these items in cash once you reach your destination. Consider some options that can help provide you with a continuous source of food:

Fishing Line - Fish is an excellent source of protein, and having some fishing line provides you with a great way to catch your next meal if you have time to stop and fish. You can often do fine with just a small spool, and the weight of the test line you choose will depend on your needs.

Fishing Pole - At first, you may think there's no way you would have room to pack a fishing pole. However, there are a number of new inventions that offer pocket-sized, collapsible fishing poles.

This can make your fishing easier.

Hook, Swivel and Sinker Set - A fishing line and pole are helpful, but without hooks, swivels and sinkers you'll have a hard time catching any fish. You only need a small number of each, so it is easy to keep the kit light.

Unless you want to trust your ability to light a fire, you may also want to consider a portable, lightweight stove. This is certainly one of those items that you can choose to do without if you need more room or a lighter pack. These portable stoves have the advantage of heating faster than building a fire, so you can boil water more quickly or prepare your meal more easily. These stoves are also good at keeping your location private since they don't produce smoke like a fire does.

However, if you are going to pack a stove, you will need to keep in mind the space and weight required for fuel. You can pack just a couple of fuel containers and use them sparingly.

CLOTHING

When it comes to clothing items, there is really only one rule to consider when packing your bug-out bag: only carry what you need for survival. Clothes take a lot of space and weigh more than you may think. So, when you pack your clothes, limit them to just a few essential undergarments.

When you bug out, you should plan to wear the same durable clothes each day and change only your undergarments to maintain hygiene. When you are bugging out, your most important thought should be survival, whether you are disappearing or running from a disaster.

Perhaps the most important clothing item to pack is a pair of socks. Your feet are very important since you don't want an infection or blisters to slow you down while you're trying to get away. You want to pack enough socks to rotate to a fresh pair each day.

It can be a good idea to consider quick-drying undergarments. These allow you to wash them and then tie them to the outside of your pack to dry. Since they are designed to dry quickly, you will likely only need to pack one spare set and rotate daily.

A sewing kit is helpful for keeping your clothes in good condition.

Lastly, make sure you have a good rain poncho. Nothing causes heat loss faster than wet clothes. A poncho is a thin, lightweight garment that doesn't take up much space and can help keep you comfortable while on the run.

5 Shelter and Bedding Options

What you choose to pack for personal shelter and bedding will largely depend on personal preference. If you have good survival skills and knowledge, you will be able to make your own basic survival shelter. However, it is crucial that you stay warm and dry whether you are outdoors or sleeping in a car. Therefore, it is always a good idea to pack a sleeping bag. Some other options to consider are the following:

1. Tarp Shelter
2. Survival Hammock
3. Sleeping Pad
4. Zip Ties
5. Paracord

4 Ways to Start a Fire

Fire is nearly as important as food and water for survival. Fire allows you to purify water, cook food, stay warm and safe. You should always make sure you pack three critical fire-starting tools and learn how to use them so you can always have a fire, no matter what happens.

1. Waterproof Matches
2. Fire Striker
3. Electrical Lighter
4. Small Magnifying Glass

16 Must-Have First Aid and Medical Supplies

Whether you are going to be in the great outdoors or staying at a hotel, first aid and medical supplies are always something you need to keep on hand. There is always a chance of illness or injury, and you want to be able to treat these issues. Even a minor cut can lead to an infection if you don't treat it properly. The following are some important things to have in your first aid kit:

1. Personal medications
2. Wound gauze roll
3. Surgical tape
4. Band-aids

5. Neosporin
6. Painkillers
7. Blood Clotting Sponge
8. Super Glue
9. Vaseline
10. Antibiotics
11. Sterile Alcohol Prep Pads
12. Hydrogen Peroxide
13. Cotton Swabs
14. Tweezers and Nail Clippers
15. Insect Repellent
16. Sun Screen

7 Personal Hygiene Must-Have Items

When it comes to survival, your personal hygiene won't include a hot shower every day, but that doesn't mean you can get rid of all your personal hygiene items. If you are going to be on the run, no matter where you are, you will want to have basic sanitation needs met. Some items you should consider packing include the following:

1. Towelettes
2. Mini-Toothbrushes
3. Mini-Toothpaste
4. Dental Floss
5. Soap
6. Tampons
7. Hand Sanitizer

6 Core Must Have Survival Tools

If you are going to be on the run or staying outdoors, there are some core survival tools that you absolutely must make room for in your bug out bag:

1. High-Quality Compass
2. Compact Folding Shovel
3. Survival Knife
4. Multi-Tool Pliers
5. Portable Solar Charger

6. Survival Hatchet

3 Lighting and Illumination Options

Lighting is something else essential to survival. Even if you are staying in your car, after dark, you need some form of light. There are a few good options for lighting, including the following:

1. LED Headlamp
2. LED Tactical Flashlight
3. Glow Sticks

4 Communication Tools You Will Need

Whether you are bugging out due to a natural disaster or you're on the run from someone, communication equipment is valuable to keep you in touch with what is going on in the world around you. Some important items to have on hand include the following:

1. Hand Crank Digital Radio
2. Protected Smart Phone

3. Signalling Mirror
4. Multi-Functional Survival Whistle

CHOOSING WHAT TO PACK

As I said before, this is a general list, and what you choose to pack will be based on certain factors. There are five things to consider when determining what to pack in your bug-out bag.

What do you know how to use

Your survival skills

Regional weather conditions

What obstacles might you face

The population density of the area you'll be travelling to

CHOOSING THE RIGHT-SIZED BAG

Once you know which supplies you will need in your bag, you can start considering the size of the bag you need. The proper bag size should be based on your torso size. Measure yourself from neck to hipbone. There are some manufacturers who have a bag designed specifically for men, women, and children, so you can find the right one to meet your torso size.

It is important to measure and get the appropriate bag because it needs to fit comfortably on your hips. While each manufacturer might be a little different in their size guidelines, a general guide is the following:

Extra small = up to 15 1/2 inches

Small = 16 to 17 1/2 inches

Medium = 18 to 19 1/2 inches

Large = 20 inches and up

Storage Space

No matter what type of pack you choose, you want one with plenty of storage and minimal wasted space. However, even if you have extra storage space, it doesn't mean you need to fill it. If you find you have extra space, leave it for future expansion and gear changes. It is more important to monitor your overall weight, since you don't want to exhaust yourself while running.

The best bag will also have several zippers, pouches and both visible and hidden storage compartments. You don't want to just randomly stuff items into your bug-out bag. Rather, you want to be able to quickly and easily access exactly what you need when you need it. Therefore, the best bug-out bag will have separate compartments for all your food, clothes and gear, organised efficiently. Some important aspects of a bug-out bag include the following:

Compression straps

Top lid

Hydration tube

MOLLE system

Hip belt pockets

Water bottle pocket

Dedicated sleeping bag compartment

Once you have gone through all these steps, you will have a good bug-out bag. However, weight is key; make sure your bag isn't so heavy that you won't be able to carry it for long distances and periods. In the end, it is important to find a bag that fits all your personal storage and survival needs.

Once you have successfully disappeared, you need to start building your new identity. Let's consider a few brief tips on how to do this.

AVOID LEAVING TRACES

Everywhere you go, you unintentionally leave traces of yourself behind. Pieces of clothing, door knobs, carpets, telephones, toilet seats; they can contain traces of you. Your skin flakes all the time. Depending on why you are disappearing and who is tracking you, these skin flakes and other traces can be used to trace you through blood type and DNA.

Once you know the risks associated with being found, you can know which of the following precautions to implement so you will avoid leaving traces of yourself behind to be found by those tracking you.

Always Wear a Hat or Cap

Wearing a hat everywhere you go serves two purposes. For one, it prevents you from getting spotted on security cameras and leaving an image of your face behind. Second, it will reduce the number of hair follicles you leave behind. This will reduce the evidence left for those tracking you. You can also choose to cut your hair really short. The goal is to limit the amount of physical evidence you leave behind that can be used to track you.

Seat Covers

Paper toilet seat covers do more than help with hygiene and cleanliness in public toilets; they will also reduce the possibility of leaving trace evidence behind. They can reduce the amount of skin, sweat and other body fluids you might inadvertently deposit on the toilet seat in public restrooms.

Avoid the Mail

Obviously, you never want to lick a stamp or envelope and leave saliva behind. However, it goes without saying that you don't really want to mail anything to anyone unless you do it anonymously. The mail is truly a major way to be found if you aren't careful.

Avoid Leaving Bodily Fluids

This can include blood, saliva, semen or menstrual discharge. If you happen to spill blood on something, it can be very difficult to clean it up entirely. Even after cleaning the surface, there will still be traces left behind that can be traced back to you.

Clean up After Yourself

If you're staying in a hotel room, be sure to wipe down every surface before you leave. If you use the bathroom at a rest stop, wipe everything down after touching. When wiping away your fingerprints and skin tissue, use soap and water; otherwise, you'll still leave smudges that can be reconstructed with modern computer technology.

Flush any wiping materials down the toilet unless you're on an aeroplane, since they go into a holding tank. When wiping surfaces down, be sure to include surfaces you didn't touch. Scientific research shows that individuals will touch objects without realising it and without recalling having touched them. The only way to be certain that you are removing fingerprints is to clean everything within reach.

Rubbing alcohol can be a good option when cleaning up after yourself. This will get the natural oils that make up the majority of fingerprints. Once you leave a hotel room, even if you've wiped it down, be sure to hang up the cleaning sign. You want to make sure the room is vacuumed, cleaned and touched up by the hotel cleaning staff as soon as possible.

Choose Where to Eat

It is best to avoid eating in restaurants when you are trying to keep yourself hidden. Restaurants are full of drinking glasses, eating utensils and other surfaces that can easily harbour a trace of you. Fast-food restaurants are a better option since you can take the food with you and not worry about leaving traces of yourself behind. Just keep in mind that most fast-food places will still have a video camera that records everyone who enters, leaves and stands in line.

Avoid Cameras

This brings us to the last and most important aspect of keeping yourself hidden and avoiding depositing traces. Don't look for security cameras, but notice where they aren't and focus on that area. When you look up at the camera, the shadows and contrast in the video shots improve. Rather, always keep your head down in areas where cameras are usually located, and avoid them.

Along with avoiding leaving traces of yourself, you also need to know how to protect your physical privacy so you don't get found by those tracking you.

COVER YOUR TRACKS

The first thing you need to do when you choose to disappear is to make sure you cover your tracks. There are four steps you need to take to ensure you properly cover your tracks and avoid your opposition finding and following you.

GET RID OF POSSESSIONS

You don't want to leave any leads behind for those who might try to follow you or find where you've gone. You want to make sure you tie up loose ends by getting rid of personal possessions, but don't do this by faking your own kidnapping. It is important that you make it clear that you vanished voluntarily. There are three things you need to do to get rid of your possessions.

First, destroy as many pictures as possible. The more recent the photos, the more important that you destroy them.

Second, abandon your car and find other means of transportation.

Third, don't take any mementoes with you. This can leave a connection to your old life and is a valuable resource for those tracking you. Anything you commonly use or have a strong connection to needs to go.

Disconnect

In today's electronic world, this is a very important step to take. Slowly decrease your online activity until no activity is normal for you. This way, people are less likely to notice when you delete your Facebook, Twitter and other social accounts. Investigators will have a hard time finding you, and they won't be able to get information from your online friends.

However, this step also takes preparation. You can't simply pack a bug-out bag and take off tomorrow. If you do this, you won't be able to disappear successfully. Rather, take the time to prepare in advance by letting go of your old personality a little at a time. If people get suspicious and you need an excuse, you can always say you are taking a break from the electronic media bombarding you.

Get Rid of Plastic

From the moment you choose to disappear, you should only use cash for everything. Credit cards are the easiest way to track a person down. Get rid of any credit cards by cutting them up or burning them. You shouldn't even keep an emergency credit card on hand to avoid the temptation to use it.

When it comes to getting rid of plastic, you don't want to just limit yourself to credit cards. This also applies to any plastic cards that can be tied to you. Membership cards, reward cards, anything that has your name on it or a magnetic strip needs to go.

Consider a form of transportation that doesn't require a driver's license, such as a bike, train or bus. However, if you choose to travel by public transportation, be aware that security footage can be used to track you. You should also avoid taking a taxi since the drivers may be more likely to remember your description and location.

Flying is also likely out of the question. Most airlines won't let you buy a plane ticket without you giving out a lot of personal information, including a credit or debit card. You certainly can't travel under your real identity. No matter where you travel, you will be tracked since airlines have the closest ties to the NSA, FBI, and other security organisations. You could try travelling with a fake identity and passport, but scrutiny of these is often intensive and difficult to avoid.

LYING

There's no way to avoid this. If you are going to disappear, you're going to have to lie to people around you. It's unavoidable and hopefully will lead to good results in the end.

The first step of lying is to create false leads. Change your address, book a flight to a place you won't go and change your name spelling. It is important to create a backstory that confuses anyone looking for you. At the same time, create a fake identity for yourself and stick to it to avoid confusing yourself with too many identities.

Since you are going to be distancing yourself from family and friends, you are going to need to lie to them. When you show up less often, they will have questions. While it is best to completely cut ties with your family and friends, there are a few ways to keep in contact with them. You can create email accounts on public computers or use prepaid phones. While people can't find you, you can still find them. Even if you stay in contact with family and friends, you should never tell anyone or give them hints about your location.

You won't be able to successfully disappear without work. You will need to get a lot of things set up early so that you can make a clean disappearance. You don't want to end up trying to set things up while on the run. It is best to prepare slowly and disappear rather than suddenly drop off the radar, which will raise eyebrows. Lastly, make sure you don't pay for a false Social Security number or passport, since this can easily get you into more trouble.

PROTECTING YOUR PHYSICAL PRIVACY

Whether you are disappearing and starting a new life or you simply want to get away from today's electronic and crime filled society, it is important that you learn what you can do to protect your physical privacy. Banks, hospitals, stores and restaurants all have privacy laws that should protect us from the unnecessary force, but this isn't always the case. If you are worried about your physical privacy, then keep reading for some tips on how you can protect it.

What impact does internet privacy have on your physical privacy? Do social networking websites do everything they can to keep your physical address private? Stalking, sexual predators, and identity theft are all dramatically increasing in society; thanks in part to social networking sites such as MySpace and Facebook. For children and teenagers, online bullying has become a major issue.

Even if you take every advantage of privacy settings both online and offline, you still have to deal with the potential for pretexting or phishing scams. Consider the following steps to ensure you are doing everything you can to protect your physical privacy.

PRETEXTING

When it comes to physical privacy, one thing you can't forget is your actual identity. Some criminals target Social Security numbers, credit card numbers, bank account information, cell phone records and other physical data. Other criminals are after your body, and they do this through a process known as pretexting.

Pretexting is when a criminal pretends to be someone else or tries to gain access to private information under false pretenses. Sometimes these individuals will even call a bank to pretend they are someone else, or you, to get your bank account number, utility account number, addresses or any other wide variety of information.

Some of the information gathered about you might be found in public records, such as whether you filed for bankruptcy or your real estate taxes. Someone you know could be inadvertently dragged into pretexting when they are lied to and think they are helping someone. It is scary to think about how much information someone can find out about you with just a few bits of information like a cell phone number, birthdate or address.

Ghost Addresses

The first step to becoming invisible is to get yourself a ghost address. There are a few options for how you can do this. For example, you can pay a small business to have them accept your mail, or you could use a Commercial Mail Receiving Agency (CMRA). Of course, you need to promise not to use the address for anything illegal. Another option is to set up a virtual address or office. The easiest option is to get a mail forwarding service.

A mail forwarding service can come in handy, especially if you want packages to be signed for while you are away from home or travelling. Sometimes mail can even be scanned and forwarded to you by email. The most popular function of these services is that they allow your mail to be delivered to any location other than a post office or home address, which makes it easier to track you.

LIVING OFF GRID

This is likely a term you've heard used before. It is often applied to those who live self-sustainably. It means individuals who produce a significant amount of their energy needs through renewable resources like water, solar or air. If you have no electric bills or other utility costs, you will make it even harder for yourself to be found. This is truly an excellent way to protect your privacy.

However, keep in mind that this is easier to do with a small home. If you can't completely go off-grid, you can choose to reduce your dependence on electricity by investing in solar panels or wind turbines. Many governments offer significant tax advantages that could even be a decent monetary investment, in addition to the privacy benefits they offer. It is very easy for any average home to go off the grid without having to adjust your lifestyle too much.

The focus is on avoiding utility consumption, so you don't have to disclose your location to utility providers and compromise your personal privacy.

PREPAID PHONES

One of the easiest ways to improve cell phone security and privacy is to use a prepaid cell phone. Drop your contract with your cell phone provider and use a prepaid service such as H2O Wireless. While you will still need to provide some information, such as a name and address, you won't have to worry about a credit report or signing a contract. Most of these phones are on pay-as-you-go or month-to-month plans. This will reduce some of the paper trails that lead back to you.

If you are worried about protecting your physical privacy, you should consider reducing your digital footprint as well. This will make it more difficult for people to find you physically. When you are aware of pretexting and take steps to resist it, such as the methods recommended above, it will make it easier for you to disappear.

A good way to protect your privacy and stay hidden while on the run is to make sure you properly cover your tracks. Let's see how you can do it.

This is just the beginning, and how you can stay hidden while on the run. However, once you reach your destination, you will need to start your new life. The first step in this process is to create a new identity.

CREATING A NEW IDENTITY

One of the most essential parts of disappearing is creating a new identity. How you obtain a new identity will depend on your reason for disappearing. For example, if you are disappearing because of spousal abuse or testimony in a trial, then a law enforcement agency will likely help you get a new identity. If you are choosing to disappear on your own, you will need to change your identity yourself or hire someone to do it for you. If you are going to create a new identity, you need to be very careful.

Nearly everyone faces some form of investigation in their lifetime, whether it is for credit, a job or a business transaction. Even if you are going to stay off the radar and avoid all of these types of investigations, you still want your new identity to stand up to the smallest investigation. If someone does a check on you online, are they going to find something, or absolutely nothing at all? Even finding nothing can make people suspicious.

It can be difficult to fabricate your own identity from scratch, but it has been done successfully. Mainly, you need to make sure there are no holes; otherwise, you will easily fail any investigation. Consider the following steps when creating a new identity.

Changing Your Name

When creating a new identity, the first crucial step is choosing a new name. You want to choose something that is easy to use and something you don't mind being called. If you want to make yourself hard to find, consider using a generic name. There are several ways you can find a good name.

Finding a New Name

While it is important that you create a genuine identity, you don't want to assume the identity of a living person. This is a mistake that can easily get you into a lot of trouble. If you copy the identity of a living individual, you will be easier to track, and if a duplicate passport or another ID is found, it can cause serious trouble for you.

Depending on your reason for disappearing, you may be able to simply look to your own past for a new identity. There are many individuals in your past who you can use as a basis for your new name. You can use someone's identity after they have died.

For those who have been in the military, you can use the name of a war buddy who either died in combat or is missing in action. You will likely also know a lot about them, which will help back up your new identity. In addition, since the death occurred outside the United States, the death was likely not officially registered in the town where the birth occurred.

For similar reasons, you can consider childhood friends who may have died young. You will already know enough about them to support a good back story. Again, if they died anywhere other than their hometown, there is likely no record of their death.

If you can't think of anyone personally who died young, you can simply take a walk through a cemetery and look at the tombstones. Some of these tombstones only contain a name, date of birth and date of death. However, the ones that include a parent's name or place of death are going to make it easier for you to get the ID you need.

Another place to look for your new identity is the newspaper's obituary column. For small towns or rural areas, this can be a great option, since you will have fewer to go through and will get more details about each individual. You can choose to use the name of anyone at the right age who died in a distant city.

It is pretty easy to find the identity of a deceased person to use, so you can even be choosy with which identity you want to take. Be sure to choose an identity that aligns with your purpose for disappearing, so carefully consider the characteristics of the identity you are considering using. Certain surnames come with advantages and disadvantages. If your name is too generic, like Smith, then a police officer is sure to look into it. In general, the best names are those from the British Isles or Northern Europe since they are fairly common throughout the United States. In addition, you want to avoid Spanish or Spanish-sounding names as these tend to be investigated due to immigration difficulties.

While choosing a name may seem like a small detail, it is often the one thing that trips up those looking to disappear and start a new life. Consider the education of the individual's identity you are taking. Perhaps they have a college degree that can make it easier for you to get a job. If not, you may need to go back to school. This can actually be a good thing, since universities can give you a chance to get used to your new identity while facing less scrutiny.

On the other hand, it is best to avoid identities that have specialised training. For example, you don't want to assume the identity of a doctor, since it requires a lot of identification, and you don't want to be called upon to use professional skills you don't really have. If possible, find an identity of someone who was in the same line of work as you, since they likely also had the same interests as you. However, if you can't find an occupational match, you want to find a general background that can be adapted to whatever jobs you need.

Lastly, you don't want to assume the identity of someone who left family behind. These individuals may be receiving Social Security or other benefits as a result of the death. You don't want to choose an identity that has any type of connection to a living individual, as this will only create more problems for you.

Once you have chosen the appropriate name for yourself, make sure you take the time to get used to it before you disappear. Get comfortable with your name by practising signing your name. Introduce yourself to some strangers using your new name to make sure it feels natural to you.

Fill Out a Petition

If you plan to legally change your name, you will need to complete a petition required by your state. On this petition, you will need to list reasons for wanting a name change. You can find the appropriate forms on the courthouse or the state court's websites.

The form needs to be notarised and filed with the clerk at the courthouse. The petition is automatically sent to a judge to ensure it clearly and completely explains your reasons for changing your name. If you are an immigrant, ex-convict, or attorney, you will need an affidavit of service of notification to the authorities along with your petition.

Attend a Name Change Hearing

Most of these hearings are fairly straightforward, with the judge just asking you a few questions. If you can answer clearly and honestly with your reasons for wanting to change your name, then you should have no trouble getting your request approved.

Change All Legal Documents

Once your name has been changed, you can use the documentation from your hearing to apply for a new driver's license or passport, and your new identification will be complete. Also, remember to use your new name on any car titles or loan documents. If you do all of this in advance, it will be easier to get a new Social Security card.

CHANGING SOCIAL SECURITY NUMBER

Fill Out an Application

The first step is to use your new name to fill out an application for a new Social Security card. You can get this form online at the Social Security website. Along with your form, you need to provide evidence of your age. This can be birth certificates, adoption papers or religious documentation. You will also need to provide evidence of your identity, such as your new driver's license, passport or non-driver identity card. If you haven't changed these documents over to your new name yet, you can provide proof of your recent name change, such as the court order from your hearing.

Go to Your Local Social Security Office

Once you have finished filling out your form, you should take it, along with the necessary proof of age and identity, to your local Social Security office to present your case to an officer. You will be offered a new Social Security number if you are able to satisfy one of the following criteria:

- You are the victim of domestic abuse, harassment, or your life has been endangered in some way.
- Sequential digits in the Social Security number are causing confusion.
- More than one person has the same number.
- There is a religious or cultural objection to the sequence of digits of your Social Security number.
- You are the victim of identity theft, and the use of the number continues to endanger you.

Contact Law Enforcement

This step may only be necessary for those who are running from an abuse situation, but if you want to disappear completely, you will likely want to avoid law enforcement contact. If you contact your local law enforcement agency, you can tell them that your life is in danger unless you get a new identity.

A law enforcement agency will be able to provide you with the documented evidence you need to have the Social Security Administration change your Social Security number.

BIRTH CERTIFICATES

Most identification in any country traces back to the original birth registration. Therefore, the first thing an identity changer needs to do is obtain the birth certificate of the original identity holder. To do this, you need to know where and when the person was born, and, ideally, their parents' names and their mother's maiden name.

Once you have the proper identification, you need to request a copy of the birth certificate. This is common enough that it shouldn't draw attention. In fact, so many people lose their birth certificates for various reasons that the US Passport Office provides guidance on how to request a certified copy.

There is often a small fee to get a duplicate birth certificate. Once you have a birth certificate, the rest of your documents won't be that hard to obtain. After you have all the documents, you can start using your new identity.

5 Ways of Using Your New Identity

Once you have a new identity, you can start your new life. There are five things you need to do in order to properly use your new identity.

1. **Start Over from Scratch**

   When you change your identity and disappear, you will have no credit or employment history. There will be no job or personal references to help get you started. You won't even have a record of education or special training. You will also need to be prepared to answer questions about any missing holes in your background.

2. **Practice Using Your New Name**

   Practice both writing and speaking your new name. You don't want to accidentally slip and use your old name. Even one slip-up can cause issues. You also want to practice using the lies you have developed about your family and personal history.

3. **Adopt new Behaviours**

In order to truly disappear and start a new life, you don't want to fall back on any mannerisms, dress or behaviours that link to your old life. Develop a taste for new foods and don't go to your usual restaurants. Consider taking up some new hobbies. You will also want to consider making small changes to your appearance, such as changing hair colour or wearing glasses instead of contacts.

4. **Move Away from People Who Know You**

You should never give any of your former friends or family members information about your new identity or location. Reduce the chances of someone recognising you by moving far away from those who can accidentally expose your new identity.

5. **Keep a Low Profile**

Depending on your reasons for disappearing and the method you choose to change your identity, both government and private entities may have a record of your identity change. If you are ever arrested, sued or attract the attention of the media, then your old identity could be made public.

Perhaps the most important thing to consider when creating a new identity is to ensure you are doing it legally. This is why you want to know the difference between types of IDs.

Paper Tripping and Fake ID's

Difference Between Paper Tripping and Fake ID's

Paper tripping, also known as ghosting, is a form of identity theft that basically involves a person stealing the identity of a specific deceased person. Sometimes, individuals who do this even steal an individual's role in society. In the 20th century, it was a very common practice worldwide. Typically, the stolen identity belonged to an individual who wasn't widely known to avoid capture, since identity theft is often unacceptable in most countries.

Often, an individual would steal the identity of someone who wasn't much older or younger than themselves. Other times, the individual may change their original identity in order to start a new life as another person.

Are the Practices Similar?

Those who want to disappear and start a new life are often confused as to whether ghosting is the same as using a fake ID. In fact, these are two very different concepts. There are certain services you can't get while using a fake ID. On the other hand, ghosting involves a person actually getting the identification of a deceased person; they aren't faking it and are obtaining a genuine identification that doesn't belong to them.

This means those who use ghosting can access many benefits, including Social Security benefits and loans, unlike those with a fake ID.

WHEN DOES IT BECOME IDENTITY THEFT?

For many years, government agencies were unable to exchange vital information, such as death certificates. When people learned of this, they took advantage of the situation. The main reason for this was the benefits available to them, including having access to a passport, social security, and bank services.

3 TYPES OF GHOSTERS

Criminals on the Run

These are individuals with a criminal record who aren't comfortable with it. They want to hide their past or reform and start a new life. They prefer to live life as a deceased person rather than be identified as a criminal. Usually, these people are fleeing their hometowns.

Irresponsible People

These are individuals who don't take life's duties seriously and want to run away from marriage, family, and other responsibilities. These are the ones who want to live big under the name of a deceased person, usually one who has worked hard and acquired wealth.

Identification

Some people want to be associated with certain people in society in order to receive benefits. For example, in South Africa, light-skinned individuals used to steal the identity of dead Caucasians in order to avoid identification under the Apartheid regime.

How Do Ghosters Get Their Information?

Most Ghosters get their information about deceased individuals through public archives. This gives them access to many candidates, allowing them to choose the best. Others choose to get their information from obituaries. In some countries, such as England, all birth, death, marriage and adoption certificates are public documents, which makes it easier to obtain a deceased person's birth certificate for an identity change.

DOES GHOSTING STILL HAPPEN?

While ghosting isn't as common as it once was, it certainly still happens today. Technology makes it easy for Ghosters to learn of a person's death and allows government departments to transfer information easily. In addition, in most states, it is a crime to become a Ghoster, and the penalties for it are pretty heavy.

Identity theft used to be common worldwide. However, today it doesn't happen as often as it did before. Ghosters have the depressing drawback of always being on the lookout. There are also additional penalties if the Ghoster is caught. It is important to keep these facts in mind when setting up a new identity once you disappear.

After getting your new identity, you need to start

building your new life. Until you can establish enough of an identity and history to rent or buy a place to live, you are going to need to know how you can anonymously check into a hotel and maintain your privacy.

HOW TO CHECK INTO HOTELS ANONYMOUSLY

Checking into a hotel anonymously and discreetly is much easier than you might think. While it may feel dishonest, wanting your privacy and deceiving people are two completely separate issues. It is completely legal to check into a hotel under a different name.

While the hotel may need to verify your identity, they will adhere to the name you registered with when booking your room. Whether you book your hotel room online, in person or by telephone, you can do so anonymously. Use the following steps to do so:

First, choose a pseudonym to use. You want an anonymous name that isn't easily noticed. This is the name you will use when registering at the hotel. For example, Oscar Wilde used the name Sebastian Melmoth to register at L'Hotel in Paris. Wilde spent his last days in the hotel, and they even arranged for his funeral.

Second, pay in cash. If you are worried about someone checking your credit card or bank account statement, then use cash. You may also have to do this if you are disappearing and on the run since you will have destroyed your credit cards and are using cash to pay for everything anyway. When you pay in cash, the only record of your stay will be the receipt you receive from the hotel at checkout. You can easily destroy this paper so that you are the only one who sees the information.

Third, ask the hotel to keep your identity private. Hotels often won't disclose information about their clients without prior consent. The hotel will likely have a privacy policy and ensure your booking information remains secure. If you are in doubt, just ask the hotel, and they will address you by the name you registered with, regardless of how you pay your bill or what name appears on your credit or bank card, or any other identity documents you provide.

Fourth, pick a hotel known for its discretion and trustworthiness. Choose a hotel that also makes you feel safe and protected. If you don't know a hotel well, then you may want to trust something out of the way.

Fifth, use a contact address that suits your needs. If you are asked by the hotel for a contact address and telephone number but want to remain anonymous, you can use a friend's or family member's address. Or you can pick any random address and phone number you've memorized. The only reason a hotel will need this information is in case there is a problem with your bill or if you leave something valuable at the hotel. In any case, it is highly unlikely they will ever use either of these to contact you.

Some general tips and warnings that you should consider when booking a hotel anonymously include the following:

- If you book online, use your pseudonym for the name that you are registering with.
- When booking online, make sure you delete your history on the computer and confirmation emails.
- Showing an identity card, driver's license or

passport at the hotel doesn't prevent you from registering under a pseudonym; the hotel will be discreet.

- Don't use a fake ID, a false address or misleading information if there is a chance the hotel will find out; otherwise, they might report it to the authorities.

Your next step will be to find suitable employment to help you start your life again and meet your basic needs.

How to Make Money While On The Run

When you want to disappear, the idea is to hide out only as long as needed, then start rebuilding your life with a new identity. When you first start out, you can get a lot of help through homeless shelters, job placement services and day labor. To give yourself the best possible chance, you want to save up as much money as possible before going on the run.

If you are hiding out in a city or town, then you stand a decent chance of finding food and staying warm. There are often shelters run by various religious groups that will be willing to provide you with food and shelter. However, sometimes these shelters can be located in dangerous neighborhoods, so you should use caution. Therefore, your best option is to find work as soon as possible.

You likely had some type of marketable skills before disappearing. Even if you don't have marketable skills, you can still find employment as long as you're willing to work hard. If you can't find work right away, you should probably consider a shelter. Being on the streets isn't a safe option for a long period of time, especially for women or children. Consider a few jobs you can do while starting a new life.

DAY LABOR

Day labor is truly hard work, but it's typically readily available. Day labor allows you to be paid in cash for the day without anyone asking questions. If you have a skill like painting or tree trimming, you may be paid more than someone who's just moving dirt around. Without other living expenses, day labor is going to at least be enough to feed yourself and maybe set some money aside for when you need to rent an apartment.

It is important to note that day labor in the United States is typically done by men who mostly speak Spanish. They are very hardworking individuals who support families. Work bosses will often return the next day and pick out familiar faces. This means competition is high in the day-labor field, making it difficult to join a day-labor group.

JOB PLACEMENT SERVICES

Most cities offer job placement services run through government programs. You will need a valid residential address and identification to use these services. If they ask for identification, you can tell them you've been living on the street and ask for a State ID card and a Social Security number to start living a normal life.

Since you don't want to be easy to contact, you will likely need to check with the office every day to see if they have something for you. Oftentimes, these offices will accept the address of a local shelter as your contact address if you have been homeless.

If you are going to go this route, you need to be careful since it is a crime to defraud the State or Federal government. A Social Security card issued to you under a different identity must be considered to be both real and honest by you. You are going to pay taxes and file income reports with your new Social Security card. If your real identity is ever found out, then people may be reasonable about the fact that you've been working as a tax-paying member of society.

FOOD WORK

Working at a fast-food restaurant could be a good option; not only do you get minimum wage, but you also get meals at a lower price. However, consider that a fast-food worker has a lot of contact with the public, so if you don't want to be seen, this may not be the best option.

Like fast food places, you can also look into working at restaurants. As with fast food, working in a restaurant is hard work and low pay, but you also get discounted meals as part of your wage. Again, the downside is working with the public and the fact that some restaurant chains will try to encourage you to join a union.

WORK FROM HOME

An excellent option for those trying to disappear is to find "work from home jobs". One option is data entry, a job in high demand. The hours are long, and the pay is low, but you can easily do it from home. Data entry often involves taking numbers and text from printed forms and typing them into a computer for 9 to 10 hours a day. At least you can work from home without having public contact and stay under the radar.

Another option is telephone solicitation. This doesn't take much skill, since you are only dialing a phone number and reading a script when someone answers. Once you get information, you type it into a database. While not all of these jobs are work-from-home, some companies allow it.

Warehouse and Factory Work

There are a number of jobs open in warehouses, distribution centers, factories, and docks. A distribution center will sort items for shipment to stores. These are often unskilled jobs that anyone can get as long as they are willing to work hard. The benefit of these jobs is that you eventually acquire skills that are in demand and can potentially work up to a management position.

Factory workers might need certain skills depending on the individual factories in the area where you settle down after disappearing. For example, clothing factories will require workers to know how to sew or operate specific machinery.

How to Find Food while on the Run

When it comes to food, you need to stay in contact with human civilization to some extent. While survival in the woods seems like a good option, you can only do so for so long. Only a handful of people have the survival skills to live off the land for the rest of their lives. On the other hand, you want to stay near a habitation area so you can work for food or get it from a shelter. You don't necessarily have to live in a major city, but at least close to some town where you can get supplies occasionally.

Unless you feel safe keeping a lot of cash on hand. You need to know what to do with your paychecks and the cash you get from work. This is where you need to consider your anonymous banking options and how to stay hidden while keeping your money safe.

ANONYMOUS BANKING

Perhaps the biggest issue with disappearing and remaining hidden is the financial aspect. You want an anonymous way to keep your money safe and to process work checks. However, this raises the question of whether you can have truly anonymous banking. The answer to that depends largely on the definition of anonymous.

It is quite possible for you to have a private bank account where certain details are kept confidential, but they can still be revealed through legally compelled requests. In the United States, it is impossible to have a completely anonymous bank account because the law requires financial institutions to know the identities of account holders.

At one time, some countries did offer truly anonymous bank accounts, such as Austria and Switzerland. These countries allowed you to open bank accounts with no identification; you were simply given a booklet and a codeword. You would need both of these items for all transactions, which meant you had to access your account in person every time. Because of local banking laws, anyone who had the booklet and knew the codeword was considered the legal account holder. This, of course, increased the risks associated with having such an account.

However, in today's electronic society, it is very difficult, nearly impossible, to have a truly anonymous bank account. This is because of the Financial Action Task Force, an intergovernmental body focused on combating money laundering. This task force has established broad legal principles requiring banks to know the identities of account holders.

In the United States, the legal requirement for this started with the passing of the Ban Secrecy Act in 1970. Then, in 2001, the USA Patriot Act was passed, which requires all banks to check the identity of account holders against a list of people who are suspected of terrorist activities.

Today, the closest a person on the run can get to anonymous banking is to set up an offshore company. This company can then open a bank account in an overseas country. This will give you an added layer of secrecy between you and your account. However, this option is expensive and can be limited by specific local laws in the country where you are starting the company and opening the account.

Don't fall for online organizations that claim to offer truly anonymous banking options. These are often risky investments or outright scams. If you are on the run and trying to start a new life, the last thing you want is to lose all your cash. Rather, let's consider how you can get and access an offshore bank account.

THE OFFSHORE BANKING PROCESS

Many associate offshore banking with people who have a lot of financial sophistication. However, it is quite possible for an average person to open an offshore bank account in just a few hours. Each offshore bank and the foreign jurisdiction you are in will have its own requirements. Therefore, you want to research your specific situation. Consider the following if you want to open an offshore bank account.

Basic Requirements

The basics of opening an offshore bank account are very similar to opening an account in your home country. You will be asked for personal information like your name, date of birth, address, citizenship and occupation. In order to verify your personal information, you will need to provide a copy of your passport, driver's license or other identifying documents that have been issued by a government agency. Banks are also concerned about verifying residence and/or physical address, as this can affect tax issues. This requirement is often satisfied by presenting a utility bill or other such document.

Since there is a wide range of different identification documents accepted by offshore banks, you often have to provide additional assurance of the authenticity of a document. In some cases, it is sufficient to have a notarized copy of certain documents. Other offshore banks require "apostilles" stamp, which is a special type of certification mark used internationally. If this is the case, then you need to visit the government office who is authorized to issue the stamp for your specific state or nation.

Additional Documents

When it comes to offshore banking, there are often a lot of additional requirements in order to open an account. Some of these requirements you may not be accustomed to. All of these requirements are in place to discourage illegal acts such as money laundering and tax fraud, which are commonly associated with offshore banking.

First, offshore banks often want financial reference documents from your existing bank showing average balances and a "satisfactory relationship." Most of the time, an offshore bank will settle for seeing bank statements for the last six to twelve months.

Second, most offshore banks want to know the nature of the transactions that are likely to take place through your account. This may seem intrusive, but offshore banking has been under increasing pressure to decrease illegal activity. As a result, many offshore banks now want additional documents showing where the money you are depositing is coming from. If your money is coming from a job, then a wage slip from your employer is often enough proof. For investment income, an offshore bank often wants proof of your investments and where they are held. If your funds are from business or real estate transactions, then you need to have sales contracts or other relevant documents. Funds from an insurance contract require a letter from your insurance company. Inheritance funds will require a letter from the executor of the estate attesting to the funds.

Setting a Currency

Unlike a domestic bank account, an offshore bank accounts allow you to choose a currency for your funds. This can be an important feature of offshore banking since it allows you to hold funds in a different currency if your domestic currency is unstable or expected to depreciate.

It is important to understand the pros and cons of holding your funds in different currencies. For example, some currencies may allow you to earn interest on deposits, but can also lead to foreign tax liability. In addition, an exchange of currencies may be needed when making deposits and withdrawals, which can be expensive depending on the fee structure and exchange rates offered by the offshore bank you are working with.

Making Deposits

Most offshore bank accounts rely on international wire transfers to move funds electronically. However, while most domestic banking electronic transfers are free, this isn't the case for international transfers. While sending a wire transfer is simple, most banks will charge an international wire transfer fee whether you are sending or receiving funds. The price of wire transfers varies by bank, so you will want to look for deals to get the best price. Unfortunately, there aren't many other options for depositing funds, since domestic checks aren't accepted in foreign jurisdictions and personal cash can be impractical for large amounts or when traveling internationally.

Withdrawals

Offshore banks often offer a variety of withdrawal options to make their services more convenient to use. Many offshore banks offer their account holders a normal debit/ATM card that allows easy access to funds worldwide. However, you still want to consider the fees for this option, since international ATM fees can be high. You can minimize fees by withdrawing large amounts of cash at once.

Some offshore banks offer the option of checks. However, most don't prefer this method for withdrawing funds. Checks will destroy the confidentiality of an offshore account. Problems can also arise when checks are drawn on a foreign account, as they may not be readily accepted.

Most find the best option is to have two accounts: one offshore and one domestic. If this is something you can do while still staying successfully hidden, then you can use electronic wire transfers for larger amounts to your offshore account while keeping smaller amounts easily accessible in a domestic account. This will give you good privacy and security while also providing the convenience of local banking services.

Despite the widespread misinformation surrounding offshore banking, it can be a simple process. Often, all you need to do is fill out paperwork, provide basic documentation and offer additional information demonstrating you won't use the account for illegal activity. The more complicated part is choosing the right currency and optimizing your deposits and withdrawals.

However, when you consider your individual banking needs and situation, it should be easy to make the right choices. If this still seems too much for you and you want to avoid banking altogether, you will still need to cash your paychecks. There are a few options for this that don't require a bank account.

CASHING CHECKS WITHOUT A BANK ACCOUNT

First, you can take the check to the bank where it is being cashed. This is the most preferred method. Take a photo ID and the check to a teller at the bank, and you should be able to cash it. Keep in mind that most banks will take a processing fee of $10.00 or more. The bank cashing the check will also try to get you to open an account with them, but you can always decline.

Second, you can cash a check at a retailer. Many large grocery store chains, franchises, Wal-Marts and 7-Elevens will cash personal or payroll checks for a minimal fee. Depending on the store, this option can sometimes be cheaper than cashing a check at a bank or at a check-cashing service. For example, the convenience fee at 7-Eleven is 0.99%, and Wal-Mart charges $3.00 for checks under a thousand.

Third, you can go to a check-cashing company. It is best to save this option only as a last resort. This is because these companies often charge the most money for cashing personal or payroll checks. However, most of these stores also offer the quickest way to get your cash and may even be open 24 hours a day. Just keep in mind that the commission at these stores is often high because they take on extra risk by cashing pretty much any check you bring them.

Lastly, you can sign the check over to someone. If you have re-established your new identity and someone you can trust who doesn't know about your disappearing act, you can have them cash the check for you. To do this, write "Pay to the order of" and the person's name, then sign below. Most banks will have no trouble cashing these checks.

A new option you can consider to keep your money safe and keep your new identity a secret is Bitcoin. Let's consider a little more about it.

How to Have Financial Privacy and Security

There are many ways your privacy can be invaded, and just as many ways to protect it. One area to look into is your financial privacy. When it comes to your personal information as a customer, financial privacy is the most important thing. You need to ensure this information remains private at all costs and doesn't leak beyond your financial institution. Many customers today face leaks that put their financial information at risk.

Many aren't aware that personal privacy is a fundamental human right. Despite this, in many States, the laws do little to nothing to protect this fundamental right. It seems nearly impossible to secure your financial privacy under the rules and regulations of most States, central banks, and corporate policies. In addition, options such as digital currencies, buying silver or gold and bartering clubs haven't gained as much traction due to the centralization of State power.

Using Bitcoin for Financial Privacy

This is where Bitcoin is a good option. Bitcoin is a digital currency that has been gaining popularity recently. Bitcoin aims to fix the problem of centralization and allows users to have greater control of their financial privacy. With centralization, the power is vested in a central body such as a central bank. However, Bitcoin's successful peer-to-peer operation doesn't allow for a central authority or third party in the case of a fundamental currency. This decentralization allows Bitcoin to stand out from other digital currencies.

No central authority issues or verifies Bitcoins. Users can generate this type of digital currency using free, open-source software. This means everyone has access to a free Bitcoin wallet and can quickly and cheaply engage in financial transactions. Once you generate Bitcoins, you can transfer them safely and securely while maintaining your privacy.

How Bitcoin Works

Bitcoin uses extremely strong encryption protocols to help minimize the risk of loss from identity thieves or hackers. Some argue that Bitcoin is a system of digital currency that is difficult to use. However, new applications are being developed above the Bitcoin protocol that make it easier to use, nearly as easy as email.

Bitcoin transactions are nearly instant. You can also make micro-transactions using a very small amount. This type of digital currency can easily be exchanged for national currency or cash in less than an hour through various exchange services.

Perhaps the best benefit of Bitcoin is that it is very difficult for governments to compromise or take control of the protocol or blockchain behind Bitcoin. While Bitcoin currency is not legally defined, it isn't illegal anywhere. Even if States try to stop Bitcoin, they will likely fail because of the open-source code. Bitcoin works to protect financial security like no other monetary innovation on the market.

However, there are some disadvantages of Bitcoin. There are those who are overly concerned about

Bitcoin's potential as a privacy-enhancing tool. These individuals don't remember that the only moral reason a State should exist is to protect human rights and that financial privacy is a fundamental human right.

In addition, Bitcoin is extremely new, and some of its applications are difficult for the average individual to handle. As more people start to use Bitcoin, it is likely to increase in value.

Lastly, the disadvantage is that all transactions are irreversible, so you need to make sure you get it right the first time.

Although financial privacy is a fundamental human right, many individuals attempt to steal financial information. Thieves, extortioners, identity thieves, rogue States, criminal gangs and other nefarious individuals are all trying to steal your information; Bitcoin is a free and open-source software that allow you to protect your financial privacy.

How to Live Under the Radar

Today, it is quite difficult to live without government monitoring. Are you tired of being followed by security cameras all the time? Do you want to get away from the city and take a break? Do you simply want to start a new life? No matter what your reason for disappearing, the most important thing is to live under the radar. As long as you stay under the radar, you stand a better chance of successfully disappearing and starting a new life. Consider some things you need to do to stay under the radar.

However, before we discuss disappearing and living under the radar, it can't be stressed enough that you plan your disappearing act carefully and have all the details planned out in advance. For about the first three months, you want to change your appearance and close out personal accounts both financial and social. Then you are ready to keep living your life under the radar with the following tips.

Leave No Trail

As we've stated a few times, you want to carry cash with you at all times. Pay for any goods or services with cash since using a credit card will lead anyone looking for you directly to you. Don't use your real name for anything. If you use documents, make sure you use a decent shredder to destroy them.

Use an Anonymous Phone

In most countries, you can purchase a prepaid mobile phone that doesn't need to be registered to a specific personal name or address. Even if you have a phone, don't use it to contact people who were close to you since detectives or private investigators will be monitoring their phones and can easily pinpoint your location. If possible, discard the sim card to your phone every month and get a new one.

Anonymous Credit Cards

It is fairly easy to get an anonymous credit card online. Once you make an upfront payment, the credit card number and card expiration date will be emailed to you so you can use it to shop online or make hotel reservations.

Become a Tourist

This is one of the most convenient ways to stay under the radar and start a new life successfully. When you do this, you can keep your finances in tax havens and spend your time in multiple countries or destinations without having to become an actual resident. In addition, tourists are often treated better than residents in some countries, so you will have the opportunity to have the life you've always wanted.

Mail Drop Boxes

When you use a drop box, you can still receive mail from anywhere without providing a physical address. This protects you from online service providers who may want to know your wealth information based on your location or other publicly available information.

Live Simply

Living simply is very important. If you live a lavish lifestyle, you will increase your exposure to external agents that want to know where your wealth comes from. The high life invites tax agents who want to know your income, and if you can't prove this, you will face charges of tax fraud.

Enhance Online Security

Before going online, always make sure your internet connection is secure, and avoid posting anything online that you don't want to see in newspaper headlines. Use emails that can't be traced back to you.

When you do these seven things, you will be able to successfully start a new life and live under the radar. This will increase your chances of staying hidden and successfully disappearing.

This is just the beginning of your disappearing act. Let's consider a brief summary of what we have learned and what we will learn in the next two books about starting a new identity and staying hidden.

How to Disappear and Live Under the Radar: A Summary

If you haven't given thought to disappearing or at least to living under the radar, consider three facts that may give you a different perspective:

The United States has 30 million-plus surveillance cameras, one for every 10 citizens.

The average American citizen is included in 200 databases.

If you want to start a new life, you need a plan to avoid being tracked.

If you are going to disappear, there are a few things you need to do in advance. Consider the following things you need to do:

Plan at least three months in advance.

Significantly change your appearance right before disappearing.

Terminate all of your accounts, both online and offline, before you leave.

Either terminate your social network sites or leave them active and use them to provide disinformation.

Delete all computer files and remove your computer's hard drive.

Get rid of all personal items, including photos, trophies, mementos, etc.; anything that ties you to your old life.

Shred all personal info with a micro-cut shredder.

Get rid of your cell phone or tablet since these can be used to track your location.

Wipe all of your info from your cell phone before getting rid of it.

Remember that there is no such thing as being off with a Smartphone or computer. If you really don't want your location tracked, you need to remove the battery.

Rather than destroying your cell phone, consider leaving it somewhere. This way, someone will pick up your phone and possibly start using it, which could create disinformation for those trying to find you.

On your first day of disappearance, there are a few things you need to do:

Avoid any of your normal patterns: change where you eat, shop and work.

Get rid of your car and get a new one that doesn't fit your style.

Completely change your lifestyle; dress and behave

accordingly.

Stay away from interstate highways.

Get rid of the GPS device in your car, or of a navigation system such as OnStar.

Make sure your tires don't have RFID chips. Some cars have these chips in their tires, and they can link to your VIN and the tires' purchase location.

Once you have started your new life, there are a few things you need to do in your day-to-day life:

Eat at non-chain restaurants.

Pay for everything in cash.

When you go out in public, be sure to disguise yourself, even if itis just with a hat and sunglasses.

Avoid going to your usual places.

Eat to-go from restaurants to avoid leaving DNA on plates/utensils/glasses.

Stay in smaller motels and pay with cash.

Use alcohol wipes to remove fingerprints.

Use a Multi-Sweep tool to look for hidden bugs and cameras.

Cover peepholes so people can't see into your room.

Sleep in a sleeping bag in hotel rooms to avoid leaving DNA behind on hotel bedding.

There are also a few things you need to do in order to stay under the radar when starting your new life:

Make only outgoing phone calls after turning off caller ID and do so only using a basic prepaid cell phone.

Replace your prepaid phone every two weeks.

When not using your cell phone, remove the battery so it can't be remotely turned on or used to track you.

Be careful what you say in cars or near windows, since laser monitoring systems can bounce off windows to pick up sound waves and record what you are saying.

Avoid being seen on infrared cameras at night by wearing a cap with LED lights on the front, which will create a halo that shields your face from the cameras.

When restarting your new life, consider the following tips:

When choosing the best place to restart your new life, you should find a mid-sized city in a not-too-cold climate. Big cities and small towns are good for anonymity, either because of cameras or because everyone knows everyone.

When changing your identity, don't just assume someone else's. This way is not only illegal but also more difficult. Rather, petition the court to change your name legally to a new and common name.

Apply for a driver's license under your new name.

- Use an RFID-blocking wallet. Most driver's licenses and passports have RFID chips, and a blocking wallet will prevent people from reading these chips and tracking your location.
- Use a new laptop when going back online and stay away from the internet at libraries.
- Use a wired connection for your laptop and turn off Wi-Fi, which is generally less secure.
- Cover you web came since these are very easy to turn on remotely.
- Install anti-keylogger software on your computer.
- Install software that reroutes your IP address so your location can't be determined from your computer.
- Be aware of government programs that monitor phone and computer transmissions for keywords and messages.
- Change your shopping habits and never use store club cards.
- Know that all food packaging now has RFID tags. Make sure these are not used to track you by repackaging food once you purchase it and throwing away store packaging in a dumpster away from where you live.
- Get a job different from your previous one, and take a night job if possible, to limit your contact with

people.

Change jobs frequently.

Create a back story for your new identity and practice it frequently. If your base is on the truth and you just change the details a bit, it will be easier to remember and more believable to those you tell it to.

Open a bank account at a small, local credit union.

Be aware of where video surveillance cameras are located.

Never contact anyone from your past.

Be aware of what activities the police now consider suspicious, such as bird watching, sketching or painting and taking photographs in public.

Be aware of locator chips that airlines can place on your bags. You can also use this as a tool for disinformation purposes and throw people off your trail.

Governments now have the technology to identify you by the way you walk, facial measurements and biometrics.

It can take seven to ten years for your old identity to completely drop off databases.

Always be on the guard against complacency.

The less you interact with technology, the easier it will

be to stay under the radar.

WIPE YOURSELF OFF THE ONLINE GRID

There are lots of reasons to disappear and go off grid. This means getting away from the entire digital world. Maybe you are tired of all the digital ads that come at you every day, whether it be work emails or social network rants. Perhaps you simply want to get away from things for a while or perhaps you want to disappear and start a new life. Either way, you will need to completely wipe yourself off the online grid.

Your reasons for going off the grid are your own. However, as you've likely learned, it won't be easy. Search for your name on the internet, and you will be surprised to see how easy you are to find. Computer IP addresses can be tracked, and this is where your problems start. Cell phones, credit card purchases, travel check-ins and even just a toll booth can trace you. Even individuals can search for your digital footprint and track your location.

If you truly want to disappear and start a new life, you will have to be prepared to go at it alone. Whether you're on the run or just settling into a less digital life, there are a few things you need to do.

LOSE YOUR CELL PHONE

As I said before, lose your phone and then, if you have to get a prepaid one, do so without giving out your identity. A cell phone is a digital bull's eye that allows people to easily triangulate your position based on your cell signal. You don't even need to make a call to be tracked due to their built-in GPS.

You can remove the battery to protect yourself when you're not using your phone. Replace the battery for a true emergency when you have to use your cell phone. You can also go on the run without a cell phone and leave yours somewhere for people to use, so it misdirects those trying to find you. You definitely don't want to get a cell phone that is difficult to access the battery.

This doesn't mean you have to go entirely without a cell phone. You can easily and cheaply purchase prepaid phones at department stores or gas stations. You can give one to someone you want to keep in contact with and keep the other for yourself. You can even purchase one without showing ID.

For extra protection, don't use your phone to make a direct phone call. Rather, use a prepaid calling card. You can also get some portable, solar-powered chargers for your gadgets, so you don't have to rely on power outlets.

USE GIFT CARDS FOR PURCHASES

You can still make online purchases even if you are disappearing and starting a new life. Use your cash to purchase a credit card gift card, such as Visa or American Express. You can get these anywhere, use them to purchase things online, and then throw them away when you are done. The transactions with these cards are between the retailer and the credit card company; your personal details aren't required, and nothing will appear on your statement.

DON'T BE SOCIAL

You will definitely have to give up on Facebook and Twitter. It is best to just walk away if you can. If not, then you will need to create anonymous accounts from a remote location. You should definitely not friend or follow anyone you actually know.

Erase Info Associated with Pictures

If you are in the habit of sending or posting digital photos, you should at the very least remove the EXIF data from the image file. This information can include the camera make, the date and time the picture was taken, and, in some modern cameras, geographical location information. With enough pictures and time, people can easily find a pattern and know where you've been and where you're likely to be going.

Encrypt Messages

You may still need to send emails on occasion. Obviously, you will need to set up a new account. Even then, you still want to make sure no one can read what you send. It is a good idea to use Gmail from Google, since it defaults to SSL encryption when you're on its website. This will help if you are using public wi-fi.

For added security, you want to encrypt any messages you send. There are a number of free open-source programs that can help you encrypt your messages.

Hide Your IP Address

The most certain way to be noticed is to visit websites that collect visitors' IP addresses. This can even be the case with some Facebook applications. Once an IP is matched to you, it is easy for law enforcement or clever hackers to call the ISP assigned to that IP and link it to you. If you are surfing from a school or business, then you can even be tracked to your specific dorm or cubicle.

A proxy server can be helpful. Tor, or The Onion Router, helps prevent people from seeing you by routing your web requests through multiple routers on the internet. While people on the other end will see an IP address for a router, it won't be your computer's IP address. Tor offers bundles for any major operating system and even some smartphones. The bundles can run from USB flash drives, so you don't even need to use your own computer.

Don't Sign In

When using free Wi-Fi, you will be asked to sign in and create an account. If possible, you want to avoid these places. On the other hand, Starbucks and Barnes and Noble have AT&T Wi-Fi that doesn't require anything more than clicking to reconnect every couple of hours. However, once you're online, you can use a VPN to help prevent wireless snoopers from seeing what you are looking at.

Don't Look for a Tail

Don't waste your time searching for a digital tail. This is a classic tactic for people tracking you, since anyone on the run wants to know how close others are to finding them. If you start going online to see what people know about you, you're likely to stumble upon a trap that will announce your location to the people looking for you. Avoid Googling yourself or posting misinformation anonymously.

Disappear and Deceive

Most of the information people find online about you comes from you. Therefore, an easy tactic is to hide in plain sight by flooding the internet with misinformation. This means you can use social networks and similar sites to spread misinformation.

While it is important to reduce your digital footprint, you still want to stay online.

Use it as a means to deceive people about where you live, your income and members of your family. This will make it harder for pursuers to find you. Consider creating an imaginary life and then start making status updates about it. The more misinformation a person gets, the more time they'll spend going in the wrong direction.

This may seem like overkill, but it shows how easily you can be tracked in today's online world. Use common sense when online and don't overshare information. Take appropriate precautions and limit what you put online.

But my advice would be to stay off the online grid at least for the first few months or till you create your new identity and you are in a safe and secure place; this way you don't sacrifice all the hard work you did last few months.

Last Words

I know I gave you a lot of information to digest, and again I tried to cover all the bases so don't think all of these should apply to you, you may need parts of it, but remember one thing, it is always better to be safe than sorry, so take all the extra precautions you need, if you take a few extra steps that will not hurt you instead those extra steps may tighten the security and safety around you and your family. Always think it through and always think twice and act only once.

If you want to learn more about how to delete yourself from the online and internet completely, check out my other book

How to Disappear From The Internet Completely While Leaving False Trails
How to Be Anonymous Online

I wish you all luck and safety if you have to go through what I have. But keep your faith and hope high, and you will come out a winner.

Good luck!

www.ingramcontent.com/pod-product-compliance
Lightning Source LLC
Chambersburg PA
CBHW071432180526
45170CB00001B/315